Praise for "G

Inspiration, affirmation, determination, and motivation are woven throughout this book through connections to multiple elements of each story. Getting to "meet" all these authors through their personal stories is a goldmine; like getting 24 new friends that encourage and empower you to succeed! This amazing book helps you recognize your WHY, highlights the value of your WHY and reminds you of the impact of your WHY. Through true stories of struggle, success, discovery, and learning, "Grow Your Why" touches your heart, makes you smile and reminds you that YOUR WHY is unique and meaningful. A must read!

Dr. Amy Mathews-Perez
Director of Special Programs, Educator, Collaborator

This talented and authentic author takes us through a process of discovery about ourselves through understanding the stories of others. By looking through the eyes of another person, we may discover parts of ourselves that will benefit us on our own personal journey of self-awareness. This book helps us to weave the valuable lessons from the stories of others so we can also define, challenge, and grow our why.

Donna M. McCance, M.ED., Educational Leader, Teacher, and Advocate for the Wellness of Humanity

---

Because education is such an 'institution', we sometimes generalize our ideas of who a typical educator is within the walls of our classrooms across the nation. The heartfelt sharing of the life stories of each of the book's contributors left me with the feeling that we each have some untapped wonder and joy in our lives. Many found anchors for their lives in the appreciation of their parents and friends who gave them a life-long inner directional for their next steps forward in their journey. Thank you, Barbara Bray, for bringing these stories to life in your new book, Grow your Why". It has taught me that we each have a unique story founded in that inner voice that grounds our choices in life—our why—and then grows it along life's journey.

Rose Colby, Competency Education Specialist, Consultant, Author of Competency-Based Education: The New Architecture for K-12 Schooling

---

Barbara Bray's "Grow Your Why" shares dozens of examples of the nuanced exploration of personal purpose. Her book is a collection of diverse stories, each a journey of self-discovery, be it in discovering, journeying, or growing one's "Why." While Bray sets the scenes at the beginning and end of the book, she stays out of the storytellers' narratives, though her presence is felt through the safe and caring space she has clearly created for them. As the storytellers share their life's paths, they discover that telling their own stories fosters a stronger, more authentic, sense of self.

Michael Bronder, Co-founder, and CEO of K12Leaders

As a self-professed Story Weaver, Barbara threads together inspiring stories from educators around the world, shining a light on the power of living life with passion and purpose. Each section of her book illustrates the journey of self-discovery, resilience, and determination in a casual, "come-as-you-are" conversation that will inspire readers to reflect on their own life journey. Grow Your Why reminds us that we can overcome any challenge placed in our path as we challenge the status quo to reach our greatest potential in personal growth. If you need a nudge to take that first step out of your comfort zone, this is the book for you!

Tamara Letter, M.Ed. Instructional Technology Coach and Author of a Passion for Kindness: Making the World a Better Place to Lead, Love, and Learn

---

"Grow Your Why" is a powerful compilation of stories from amazing educators. Reading their stories, the 'how' behind their 'why' allows educators of all levels of experience and concentration to center themselves around their own story. As I dove further into each personal element shared by these great people, I found myself reflecting on my journey, seeing awesome connections with others, and getting my soul ignited with passion. A must read for all educators!!

Dr. Darrin Peppard, author, speaker, publisher, and founder of Road to Awesome, LLC

Grow Your Why… One Story at a Time

Copyright @ 2024 Barbara Bray

Published by Why Press Publishing
https://whypresspublishing.net
Oakland, CA

This book is available at special discounts for bulk purchases of 10 or more for use as *premiums*, promotions, fundraising, and educational use. For inquiries and details, contact the publisher at info@whypresspublishing.net

Paperback ISBN: 979-8-9894945-0-7
eBook ISBN: 979-8-9894945-1-4
Library of Congress Control Number (LCCN): 2024909609

Cover design by Barbara Bray
Support from Jillian DuBois
using Canva Pro version

Grow Your Why
One Story at a Time

Barbara Bray

WHY PRESS

This book is dedicated to all
the inspirational storytellers
who share their hearts
with the world.

Table of Contents

Preface

*"We are all storytellers. We all live in a network
of stories. There isn't a stronger connection
between people than storytelling."*
~ Jimmy Neil Smith

I have been on a magical journey since I started the Rethinking Learning podcast in 2017. The purpose of my podcast was to learn about the stories of people who inspired me. The magic was when many of my guests shared stories they had never told anyone else before. Or when they shared the deeper meaning behind stories we may have known. When I heard that they were sharing something very personal, I would pause the recording and remind them that the podcast would be available online for everyone and anyone on the Internet. I asked them if they were sure they wanted to share their story. Everyone said YES. It was such a privilege to be in that moment with each guest and hear about an event or experience that changed their lives.

All of us have stories. Not just one. If we live a life of struggle and risk-taking or experience difficult or amazing events, we have many stories that shape and change us as we grow. I believed that starting a podcast would help me become a better listener and interviewer. It did, yet I'm still learning.

After a bit, I decided to do a pre-podcast planning session with each of my guests. This is when I don't record. I actively listen to the story behind the stories. That's where I got it. That time was simply about getting to know each other. It was about building a relationship with each guest, so they felt comfortable on my virtual porch. Also, we had time to discuss that personal story they may really want to share.

Long ago, I found that I enjoyed building relationships by connecting educators with other educators.

The one experience that stands out to me about connecting people happened in the early 1990s. I was at a conference, standing at an intersection in the exhibit hall, when a librarian I knew walked up to talk. Then, another librarian stopped to say hello. They didn't know each other, so I introduced them. It wasn't long before another librarian who didn't know the other two stopped to talk with me. I introduced them to each other. They had so much in common. I enjoyed listening to their conversations, but it was best for me to walk away. It felt good to connect them.

Through years of multiple experiences of building relationships with people who have similar interests made me aware of my purpose at that time: connecting people.

When I started my podcast, my purpose was to learn how to listen deeply to the stories of people I knew or who I wanted to know more about.

When I wrote "Define Your Why," my purpose was to share stories that inspired me so I could inspire others to tell their stories. It all started coming together: connections, stories, and purpose.

Through the conversations on my podcast, I connected to stories I heard from inspirational people. Each story in this book is from guests on my podcast: barbarabray.net/podcasts/

Themes are woven through the book with multiple stories from different people. With over six years of podcasts and connecting the stories, I now call myself a Story Weaver.

That's my purpose for this book: curating the stories and weaving the themes throughout those stories.

There are three sections to this book where individual contributors were posed a question in the section they chose. Each contributor has their own chapter in one of the following sections with a story about their WHY.

Section 1: Define Your Why

What story defines who you are and your why?

Each story is about what they discovered about themselves and what they were passionate about that made them realize there was a purpose for them to be here.

Section 2: Journey Your Why

What story challenged you to choose another path on your journey to your why?

Each story is about something that surprised them along their journey, gave them a reason to get up each morning, and the process they went through to redefine their purpose.

Section 3: Grow Your Why

What story empowered you to go out of your comfort zone to grow your why?

Each story is about how they were challenged to push themselves, redefined what they were passionate about, and how they advocated for their purpose.

There is a powerful connection that comes from reading about someone's memories and lived experiences. Storytelling matters. All our stories are crucial to being here and to our own existence. They extend our lives and deepen our connections.

The contributing authors chose to share a story that made a difference in their lives. In each story, you will hear the author's heart as you read and listen closely to decode a deeper story that had to be shared. I am grateful to these amazing authors:

Section 1: Define Your Why contributing authors:
Craig Shapiro, Celeste Endo, Dr. Walter Greason,
Dr. Ilene Winokur, Traci Browder, Melisa Hayes,
and Jillian DuBois.

Section 2: Journey Your Why contributing authors:
Rich Simpson, Nicole Biscotti, Hedreich Nichols,
Erika Sandstrom, Charles Williams, Dr. Jennifer D. Klein,
Noa Daniel, and Kecia McDonald

Section 3: Grow Your Why contributing authors:
Dr. Sarah Thomas, Evo Hannan, Livia Chan,
Dr. Sheldon Eakins, Stephanie Rothstein
Rachelle Dené Poth, Rita Wirtz, and
Federico Josué (Josh) Tovar

All the links the authors mentioned will be available with their names and chapters on <u>whypresspublishing.net</u>.

The themes that weave through all the stories will touch your heart. Each story touched mine. In fact, many of the stories from the **contributing** authors clarified what it means to have a sense of belonging and why they are here. What I learned is that our lives are complex, with multiple stories that change us as we grow. Stories change when we discover our purpose or when our purpose changes. We are all humans with real experiences, emotions, connections, and a purpose that defines us. Our stories are unique and personal for each person telling them. It is a real honor for me to share their stories with you.

Enjoy the journey to grow your WHY with each story.

Barbara

"Stories change people more than information ever will. Stories are the gateway to empathy."
~ Brandon P. Fleming

Section 1

Define Your Why

What story defines who
you are and your why?

In this section from the contributing authors, the stories are about the seed planted that empowered them to discover more about themselves. They share what they are passionate about and what helped them determine the reason why they are here.

"When you know your why,
you'll know your way."
~ Michael Hyatt

1

The Boardwalk is Cold in April

Finding the right path in life isn't always easy.
With persistence, passion, and perseverance,
that path will find its way to you.

G rowing up near Atlantic City was a blessing and a curse. I had the chance to visit the beach frequently with my parents and get Kohr's custard, which was a special treat I always enjoyed. My father, on the other hand, was obsessed with memorabilia, which began way before I was born when he worked there. He was always collecting a vast mishmash of all things boardwalk related. Our home was a hodgepodge collection of Atlantic City artifacts, from pictures to silverware and everything in between.

My mother and I would constantly say, "Please stop bringing home stuff!" To no avail, my father did not listen. Regardless, life continued uneventfully for quite some time. Graduations, jobs, family dinners, holidays, dating, summers spent down the shore. But then, of course, as happens in life, some things took a turn. My mother passed away after a long trial of complications from diabetes, and our family became just my father and me. Luckily, I had just gotten engaged, and my father loved my fiancée, who also happened to be a support to my mother during her illness fiancée, who also happened to be a support to my mother during her illness.

A short while after our engagement, my father discovered he had cancer. Initially, the doctors were able to treat it with chemotherapy, and he went into remission. At about this time, I accepted a position as a health and physical education teacher at a suburban school where I still teach. Prior to that, I had the same position but at the elementary level in a city school. While I loved the position and the people, I was unable to coach there.

The transition from elementary to secondary was challenging, and there were initial moments when I thought I might not be cut out for the job. My father always encouraged me to accept the challenges and to stay positive.

Those words resonated with me, especially as that first year was extremely stressful. My wife and I got married. Things started going better. The next school year came. I began coaching and was enjoying things more. My wife and I bought our first house. However, towards the end of that year, my father's cancer came back. In the beginning, it wasn't horrible, but there were definite signs of it progressing. Even with the disease, my dad stayed positive and enthusiastic. That April, though, it became clear that his cancer couldn't be cured and that spending quality time together was essential. As I mentioned earlier, I'd lost my mother a few years prior and wanted to ensure that my wife and I enjoyed quality time with my dad. Because of his love of Atlantic City, we decided to take a day trip down the shore.

While April isn't usually cold where we live, on this day, the shore was windy, with a deep, biting chill to the air. Even with the cold and wind, at my father's request, we decided to walk on the boardwalk. It was quiet and peaceful, even with the frigid temperatures. Because of my dad's illness, he struggled to walk, and we often had to slow down or stop briefly, though he denied any difficulty and insisted we keep going to clearly take it all in. It was hard for me to hold back tears, not only from my sadness but also because he kept smiling. He clearly was enjoying the time together even when it was most challenging.

I remember saying to him, "Dad, we can stop and go inside if you like. It's not a big deal. It is pretty cold!" He responded, "No, Craig, I'm so happy that you and Kyle brought me here. Let me take you out to lunch." Because my father was always one to give, even when he didn't have it, I knew arguing this point would be a fruitless endeavor.

One of his favorite spots was a famous hoagie restaurant in Atlantic City called "the White House." As we sat and ate hoagies, I thought long and hard about the experience my father was going through and how, no matter the situation, he kept a bright, positive light on things. It also made me think deeply about my life experiences and what I wanted to stand for. While I was generally a positive person, this time spent with my father and wife helped me see things in a different light.

While walking on the boardwalk and eating, I pondered what was truly important: how I wanted to treat people, my moral compass, and what my legacy might hold one day. Because of my career with young people, it struck me that "my why" was grounded in helping to promote wellness, positivity, respect, and high expectations.

In retrospect, this short trip became a pivotal point in my life. I'd be lying if everything changed in that one moment.

Nonetheless, it opened me up to new ideas and gave me a powerful perspective on life and my career as a teacher. For example, before that boardwalk trip, I'd never thought too deeply about the impact of education on children. Sure, I always knew how important learning was as I did become a teacher. But, beyond just the learning, the power we had as educators seemed to be about designing content, assessing students, and other lessons around teaching. Even though I still feel those are important today, I put a much greater value on bridging those connection gaps that are so often lacking.

My initial "why" from above still holds today. In addition, growing that why has been a foundation of my career from that cold, windy day on the boardwalk.

As you ponder your own "why," please consider this important idea.

If your role is in education, students are coming to us with successes, problems, stressors, and life events that contribute socially and academically to their progress. As we think about our own stories, we must also think about theirs. While I don't believe that a perfect solution exists for dealing with all that education brings us, here are seven of my Shap's Tips!

1. My father's health struggles gave me perspective on taking each day at a time. In our classrooms, no two days will be the same. Embrace the good ones. Don't get stuck and harp on the tough ones. Smile through them. They won't last forever, and something can be learned from those experiences.

2. The simple things make a big difference. Education tends to gravitate towards the one big "change" that needs to happen.

That rarely occurs. Instead, focus on those small moments that matter. When students excel on an exam, they greet you at the door or laugh at the silliest things. They matter! Oh, and payout compliments...to everyone over time. Those complements change culture for the better.

3. Stick it out and stay positive! Again, relating to my story above. While my father did pass away, he had a stick-withit attitude in the toughest of times. Reflect and focus on the positive things. Seek help and ideas when needed but build on the positive. Frequently, you'll find that the good really does far outweigh the bad this way. Remember, good things (aka lessons, appreciations, connections) can come from the bad/trying times.

4. Please get out of your room! The four walls may bring comfort, but they also deny us the chance to meet other amazing educators. Also, being in the hallway when students pass by is a game-changer for making connections.

5. Make time for yourself outside of work! Earlier in my career, I was totally consumed with my job. The eight-hour day often turned into twelve. I felt proud to be so dedicated. Unfortunately, too many other things suffered. I won't delve deep into them, but please trust me on this. Keep a balance with work, home, and your social life.

6. Plan, but don't plan! Yes, planning your daily lessons gives us and our students structure. It's necessary for success. With that said, avoid being so inflexible that you miss important moments with students or can't change directions. A great question, conversation, funny joke, or a hundred other "things at the moment" show a degree of authenticity that builds connections.

7. Finally, enjoy being with your students. I've known and taught others who focus on the one difficult student, the one disruption, or the one poor administrative decision. This leads to a sense of dread going to work and will impact students in negative ways, even when they aren't obvious. No job is perfect 24/7, and education is no different. With that said, being in schools and classrooms has impacts on millions of young people each day. No other job can say that!

Each of us who enter the field of education usually knows "why" we begin such an important journey. For some, it might always stay the same, and for others, it will change because of the circumstances that life brings us. I encourage each of you, no matter what job or situation you are in, to spend time growing your "why." As I think back to the time spent on that boardwalk, it's easy for me to see how my "why" has flourished. I hope the same happens to each of you.

CRAIG SHAPIRO

Craig Shapiro has been a teacher, coach, and mentor for 36 years. He started his career at the elementary school and transitioned to the high school so he could coach. For the last 28 years, he has been at the same school in Bucks County, Pennsylvania. With his teaching background, Craig found that providing people with clear, positive, and authentic information is the best way to promote education and learning. He feels blessed to be in the noble field of education. Meeting students each day is transformative for him and, hopefully, those students whom he interacts with.

Craig has been married to Kyle for 26 years. They have two children, Alana, who is just graduating college, and his son, Cole, who is currently a Junior at UNC Wilmington in North Carolina. They also have two dogs, Bella and Zoey.

Along with education, Craig's passion has always been wellness and helping others. It's one of the main reasons that Health and Physical Education is the field he chose in college. Besides teaching wellness, Craig is a competitive powerlifter and a trainer.

Craig recently launched his first book on education, "Dream Big: Stories and Strategies for a Successful Classroom." He's also excited to share his podcast: "Cutting the Crap with Shap."

To connect with Craig for any speaking engagements or to chat, go to https://www.cmsdreambig.com or on Twitter (X) @Shapiro_WTHS

The Rethinking Learning Podcast Episode #101:
Making a Difference in the Lives of Every Student with Craig
https://bit.ly/episode101-shapiro

2

Growing Great Generations

"Every generation has the obligation to free men's minds for a look at new worlds... to look out from a higher plateau than the last generation."
~ Ellison Onizuka

As a child, I had the incredibly good fortune to be born into a goofily loving family. Three generations lived in one home: grandparents, parents, my brother, and me. My grandpa, Paul Kameo Shimizu, loved singing karaoke with exuberant passion. He neatly kept an organized array of all his cassette tapes with his best songs and his proudly recorded practice sessions! One of his go-to karaoke songs was Man of La Mancha's The Impossible Dream, especially because he heard it was also the favorite song of our family hero and role model, Ellison Onizuka. In a deep voice uncannily uncharacteristic of my gentle grandpa, he would belt out the Impossible Dream in high hopes of inspiring our family.

My grandpa knew the power of education. He was the smallest in stature of all his brothers in a family of nine siblings, yet he excelled as a learner and incredibly found a way to be voted class president every year! After considering ministry, he became a history teacher, then a counselor, and eventually a Leilehua adult school principal. Grandpa was proud when both

11

of his daughters, Mom Pauline Nagata and Auntie Joyce Masaki, followed in his footsteps to become teachers. Grandpa even told me, "Celeste, I think you would be a good teacher."

After retirement, grandpa excelled at his new journey with Grandma Doris to lovingly care for my brother Todd and me, plus give my parents heart working time to grow their careers and get a bit more rest at home. I have fond memories of grandpa dipping his hands in salted water to make the yummiest musubi rice balls with day-old rice and lots of love as grandma prepared the most glorious local foods. Grandma and Grandpa also loved to spoil us with special treats of McDonald's ice cream or French fries!

School was not like home; I struggled as a student.

Stru-u-uggled!

Kids can be cruel while trying too hard to be funny. I got bullied plenty. They called me "Shrimp" and "Skittles Bite Sized Candy". Relentlessly, I was the chosen "IT!"

I suffered from low self-esteem and once hysterically screamed at my mom, "Why did you have to have me? I wish I was never born!"

Thankfully, my mom was understanding and immediately forgave my immature rants. I will always regret those most unkind words, as I now see how my mom was a nurturer, a people gardener, with a wonderful way of turning despair into two thumbs-up positivity. Extreme challenges often make us more empathetic and tuned in to how we treat others.

Little did I know back then that I would grow to have so many wonderful encounters with inspiring people along the way. As my friend Matt Tom says, "okagesama de". It is an old Japanese saying that means, "I am what I am because of you."

In elementary school, my dad would tell my family that his cousin was going to be an astronaut. I thought, "Yeah, right, Dad, ha-ha!" I was stunned when, a few years later, my family got to take a trip to Kona to celebrate the return of the space shuttle discovery. My neighbor island cousins and my family got to sleep in the back of the Onizuka Store on a row of metal framed cots. My grandaunt even let us choose one item from her store. For years, I had been embarrassed about my family's Buddhist roots. I was such an overwhelmed minority in my school. Yet I was quite amazed when I learned that intelligent and kind Astronaut Ellison Onizuka was a Buddhist, too! It made me proud of who I was and less embarrassed by being in the minority.

I had amazing peer role models to get past bad days and gift me visions of better ways. I saw how my cousin Shelley Yorita and classmate Christina Oshiro were easily outgoing and made friends with all kinds of people. Like my grandpa, they were chosen as class presidents. They were genuinely kind to everyone! I hoped to one day be like them. As my grandpa was passing away, I made a tearful promise to him that I would try my very best in school and life to make him proud. In my mind, I knew I somehow wanted to push myself to be more like Shelley and Christina.

A favorite story my grandpa told was the Tortoise and the Hare, especially since his middle name, Kameo, means turtle in Japanese. I remember that even though he was often the smallest man in a group, his actions moved mountains. After he passed away, my grandma gave me a heirloom "honu"

Hawaiian bracelet with a ring of turtles and "heart Grandma" inside. I wear it with pride every day, knowing that it is quite possible for late bloomers to blossom vivaciously when kindly nurtured and given the opportunity.

Throughout my life, my parents have inspired me. I might not have appreciated them early on, but as I continue to grow up, I have come to realize just how precious my family is and how jackpot lucky I was to be born into my family. When I was a child, every summer, my parents would take me and my brother to summer festivals all over Hawai'i called bon dances. We would go bon dance hopping! My dad would later go on to run weekly temple Wednesday night bon dance classes.

Flash forward to 2003; it was time for my own father to be a grandpa. He apprenticed under Sensei James Kunichika, under a grant from the State Foundation for Culture and the Arts, to learn Iwakuni songs and sing at the summer bon dance festivals. Lucky for this overtired teacher, he would practice his songs while calming his baby granddaughter in the wee morning hours on his reverberating chest (or was it his tummy)?

Helping to grow my why is my father, Ralston, and my two children, Chelley and Jackson. Here they are at a bon dance, a popular summer festival that happens at many Buddhist temples in Hawaii and in many Japanese communities around the world.

When I started at Queen Ka'ahumanu School, I thought I would not know a single person. Then it was like a Surprise Party as all kinds of people from my past experiences seemed to pop out of everywhere on campus to say "Hi!" I found my people and my place for me to grow!! I knew a bunch of teachers from my favorite role model, cousin Shelley; many of us shared the same Kalani High alma mater, and there were friends I knew from jazz and hip-hop dancing!

I've loved to dance since my childhood and was an eager dance student. One day, I crazily thought, if my burly father could confidently run a weekly dance class with all my dance training, maybe I could lead morning dancing for everyone at my school! After breakfast, we would gather on the basketball courts to stretch and do a bunch of hip-hop dances with simple moves I'd choreograph with our "littles" in mind. What I didn't imagine was how popular morning dance would get with all kinds of kids.

With 53% of our school population being English Learners (as of 3/29/2023), Queen Ka'ahumanu Elementary has richly diverse cultures and students who come from so many different backgrounds! Dancing would instantly bring students together because they could follow the motions without speaking a common language. No need to say, "Put your right foot in, put your right foot out." Kids could easily see and copy our motions! English Learners and special needs children could unite with all their peers on the dance field for a true melting pot of creative exercising goodness.

Dance has become a beautiful bridge for our diversity of learners and cultures. In 2013, when we first started the Wednesday-Friday morning dance at Queen Ka'ahumanu School, a little girl would come up to me daily and eagerly ask, "Esses ai? Mrs. Endo Esses ai?" Through gestures, she explained that "esses ai" meant dance. Her ELL (English Language Learner) teacher was amazed to see her dancing because she was so shy and hesitant to speak in ELL class.

I tried so hard to connect with her and asked her to repeat "esses ai" to me multiple times so I could pronounce it correctly in her language. Years later, when that little girl grew into a confident fifth grader and co-emcee of the end-of-year English Learner program, I again asked her to say "esses ai" so I could check my pronunciation. She said confidently, **"exercise."**

Wow, all that time, we had been trying so hard to communicate one word in each other's spoken language. That was just learning one single word! I can never fathom learning a whole new language in a year and taking a standardized test in it! Fortunately, the language of dance had almost immediately laid a bridge for us to connect with. Though it might take years for our newcomer students to master the English language, some learners might be able to make an instant connection through movement!

A few years into our Wednesday through Friday morning dancing, I was taking Computer Science Fundamentals, which had a dance loop lesson. In an "aha" moment, I realized that we could weave dancing into our computer curriculum! Kids could code dance algorithms together! Code Yo' Choreo was born!

When students come back to visit or people see me in the community, they often ask if we still do morning dance. I tell them we no longer dance after breakfast, yet we totally are bringing dance parties into computer science classes!! In Code Yo' Choreo, students can creatively dream up their own dances and dance loops, and we annually have code dance parties in many classrooms. Our favorite computer science curriculum, code.org, came out with its dance party lesson that completely connects to our love of code dancing!! Our older students dream up their dances in code.org/dance, and they inspire other students, especially our littlest coders!

Education Week.
Everyone is welcome! You're invited too!!
https://bit.ly/hidanceparty

Annually in Hawai'i, with the help of many people, we host a state-wide virtual computer science dance party for families. We had our first during Covid 2020 to bring smiles and active dancing to keiki, teens, and their 'ohana at home. Each year,

I've been fortunate to get my students and families to join the Family Code Dance Party, and we invite schools around Hawai'i. We are growing and getting bigger.

In 2022, we've had participants from other states join us! It happens during the Hour of Code and Computer Science.

Since the days of COVID lockdown, I have helped my school normalize goofy large, over-our-head rainbow K-drama hearts, air hugs, sparkle fingers (my friend Mili taught me), and more. Now, I get surprised each day as students call me from behind, "Mrs. Endo, Mrs. Endo!" to get a reaction from me. Naturally, I'll respond with energetic nonverbal motions like gigantic rainbow hearts. As these joyful nonverbal motions spread at school, hopefully, this kind of positivity is spread to families in our homes, too. At my own home, I love throwing and catching big bouncy Tigger-like air hugs that make this Tutu run to the bathroom to go shi-shi soon after.

My calmly supportive husband Steve and I share the delightful roles of parenting. As people sometimes wonder how I have so much energy, my husband has stuck with me to calm the storms. Together, we are growing our greatest gifts, our children, Chelley and Jackson. I am always learning something new from them, and they have taught me lessons that have helped me grow. They teach me unconditional love and how a parent cherishes their children so very much. I look at each of the incredible students who I get to teach and remember that each of them has someone who thinks the world of them, loving them to the stars and back again. Knowing that makes me want to do my very best for each cherished child.

During Covid, it was tough trying to reach out to kids through computer screens and get them eager to learn. One isolated day, I thought, since we are all confined to our homes, let's make the most out of the abundant resources all around our homes, the recycled boxes, plates, and utensils that many of us have at home. I first came up with a bit.ly/homeboundless video to share our possibilities from home. Then, I came up with an idea for Tutu Tinkerella, like comedian Frank De Lima's Tutu character. Tutu means aunty in Hawaiian; I would tell my students. Then, the next week, in horror, I realized that Tutu means grandma, and I quickly virtually visited classes to apologize and explain that Tutu means grandma in Hawaiian. Since that apology, Tutu Tinkerella has become a beloved character at our school, as the cousin of Tinker Bell and Cinderella who loves to tinker and make things with children.

As I get ready with my father to take my own son to meet our Maui Island cousins, who we rarely get to see, I wonder what new adventures we will have. We will get to stay in my Aunty

Earlyn's home, and my son will get to meet a hilariously clever, smart, and kind family for one of his first times. As I sing to my grandson, I notice that many of the songs I remember and choose are all about the richness and diversity of people. My family laughs with me as my bad memory often has me goofing up pop cultural sayings, yet lyrics to *Colors of the Wind*, *Wonderful World*, and *The World is a Rainbow* easily flow from my memory bank. Songs that speak of diversity, acceptance, and valuing of all people are songs I recall most from my childhood and have become my go-to favorites to soothe my screaming infant grandson and get him calmly cooing.

Yes, you read correctly. This Tutu has become official!! In 2023, my daughter gave birth to a son. Welcome to our world.

Won't you come on in, little Smiley Cekai? My dad, now Great Grandpa Ralston, winked from the universe and realized that the word Cekai (Sekai) is found in the Japanese song for Tortoise and the Hare, my grandpa's favorite story to tell! After all, my grandpa, Paul Kameo Shimizu's middle name, "Kameo," is also found throughout the song's lyrics.

> *"Moshi moshi kame yo kame-san yo,*
> *Sekai no uchi ni omae hodo ..."*

Just by chance, last year, the incredible Ka'ahumanu students from my mentor Diane Murakami's *Passport to Japan* class extraordinarily retold "Usagi to Kame- The Tortoise and the Hare" and sang the Japanese song schoolwide. It is quite amazing how we are all interconnected in this world.

As I listen to my son sing his favorite songs from his bedroom and hear my daughter sing to her infant son, I wonder, 40 years from now, what songs they will sing to inspire the next generation?

Questions to Ponder

1. What are some of your own cultural experiences that have rooted your purpose?

2. Who are the role models in your life who have inspired you to change for the better?

3. How can we use big, vibrant, non-verbal motions to connect with people?

CELESTE ENDO

Celeste Endo is a mega fan of teachers and the students we get to reach. She is an amateur researcher of goofy social experiments to see how people react to flying air hugs, Sparkle Fingers, Mili stars, huge rainbow hearts, jumping for joy, and wrapping around a blanket of aloha hugs. She finds these methods spark smiles and brainbow connections with humankind.

These styles and connections started for Celeste in Esther M. Goto's 6th grade class when she starred in a class film. Each child who got a starry picture in the Director's chair mattered and had an incredibly fun time! Miss Goto's class shifted life trajectories for Celeste toward better paths.

Celeste graduated from the University of Hawai'i with a Bachelor's in Elementary Ed in 1996 and a Master's ETEC in

2000. She is the 2020 KMR Complex Area Teacher of the Year and a 2022 HawaiiKidsCAN Legislative Champion, & 2022 Making IT Happen Hawaii co-winner.

Celeste is grateful to have presented at Schools of the Future Conferences, Kam Schools EdTech Conferences, Grow With Us 808 Conference, Peer 2 Peer, iTeach808, Hawai'i STEM Conference, Teach for America Hawai'i PD Day, Girl Scouts of Hawai'i Virtual STEM Fest, CSTA Hawaii Computer Science Summits, Emergency Home Learning Summit, (not just a) Green Screen Summit, faculty meetings & best of all classrooms filled with students!

Twitter (X): @celyendo
Instagram & Threads: @celesteyendo
Video: https://bit.ly/brainbowconnections
YouTube: http://bit.ly/celesteendo
Rethinking Learning Podcast Episode #135:
We Learn from Everyone
https://bit.ly/episode135-endo

3

Pain, Joy, and Creating a Shared Purpose

DR. WALTER GREASON

Move from failure to failure with no loss of enthusiasm.
~ Bill Duke, Filmmaker

When asked to "Define my why," it is important to understand that the sense of legacy and loss that my family and community have experienced shaped my individual sense of purpose from my earliest memories. My people were farm workers, often living in stables alongside goats, chickens, and horses for most of the twentieth century. My closest relatives were routinely whipped and beaten as part of their daily labor as late as 1977. Enslavement is not an abstraction for me. Segregation is not an academic debate. Anti-Black racism is as real to me as my breath, my blood, and my body. This reality is the key to the definition of my "why."

PAIN

I taught a course titled "Collective Racial Violence in American History" in 2002. It required eleven years of preparation before I could convince anyone to allow me to teach it. For almost sixty years, most Americans allowed themselves to believe that African Americans were not fully human beings. White Americans believed (deeply) that Black Americans were less intelligent, morally inferior, and prone to violence. No one dared to assert the opposite – that white Americans had been perpetrators of massive violence against African Americans for decades, if not centuries.

In those eleven years of preparation, I came to understand the pain that caused me to cry when I first heard Rev. Dr. Martin Luther King, Jr.'s "I Have a Dream" speech. That education gave me a new perspective on the century of work required to simply assert that the dehumanizing stereotypes of African Americans were carefully designed (and constantly reinforced) propaganda. I forged that pain into a sword and shield of spiritual and psychological strength to storm into the institutions that maintained the myths of white supremacy. No matter how much damage I took from the gatekeepers and defenders of the status quo, I would die before I let those lies continue unchallenged.

At every stage, there was opposition to any effort to advance civil and human rights. Cowards and their terrorist cousins always appear when social change begins to happen. The worst, however, were the people who proclaimed neutrality, objectivity, and passivity. Whenever there was a chance for enduring progress, they would betray the work at the last crucial moment. Most often, these betrayals came from places of jealousy and selfishness. The hardest lessons for me have been learning to discern who truly embraces the vision and ideals of a better world and who just wants more resources for themselves.

The work **was** and is its own reward. I have paid, and continue to pay, a massive cost for this thirty-year mission. Scarred and broken in every part of my body, my soul does not relent. The pain is real, but it is also a reminder that I can, I must, and I always will overcome.

JOY

With the loss of both of my parents and much of my birth family over the last twenty years, it is hard to explain the sense of joy that keeps me centered on my mission. My two sons, at opposite ends of adolescence, remind me that much of my time has passed and that their time is truly the next stage of our shared victories. I also look to the beloved community that I enjoy among the many authors and contributors to this volume. I immerse myself in the dynamic social universe of educators and scholars who build better worlds every day. I meditate on the visionary artists who share the deepest parts of their artistic visions with me.

As a young man, I studied the nineteenth century transcendentalists while also learning and teaching religious texts from a variety of ancient traditions. In my best moments, I reach these moments of **ecstasy**, especially in the classroom. Many of my colleagues speak about their nervousness at the beginning of a new academic year. For me, it has become excitement. The joy of connecting with students and colleagues in new ways is the best part of education.

Since starting school, I have been in educational settings almost constantly. Formal schooling for eight to ten hours per day. Another round of community education programs in the evenings for two to four hours in the **evenings** and on Saturdays. A full twelve-hour day of religious instruction shaped every Sunday. Through middle school and secondary school, I worked at least eight weeks every summer in teaching and counselling settings. At age 18, I started designing educational research projects and taught my first college class just after turning 21 years old. For another decade, every job involved lesson and unit planning, educational counselling, administrative oversight, and research into collaborative, interdependent learning. Having taught over 7,000 students to this point, it is their joy that keeps me energized in this work.

One of my favorite memories is when a student was late to class and shouted at the top of his lungs, "You started without me!" We had been working for weeks on a project that required independent research, and he **was** exuberant in his determination to share his work. More than a decade later, I still see his passion and intensity in doing the work we started in the class that semester.

When I do my best work, all the participants share in this enduring joy. It becomes a light that shines permanently within them. It is a passion that so many continue to share with family, friends, and **communities** throughout their lives. The most dramatic impacts come with students and colleagues who have the greatest pain. They have chances to heal and recuperate through these educational experiences. As a result, their own joy is profound and enduring. A passion for justice and equity often emerges as they become determined to share the joy with others.

SHARED PURPOSE

The question of 'why' is a question of purpose. When I teach about the different disciplines of inquiry, I help students to discern between the 'how' techniques and the 'why' techniques. 'How' teaches a range of approaches that are deductive, drawing inexorably towards single conclusions. They are vital skills, especially in the areas of science and social science, but they are not the totality of education.

'Why' techniques investigate larger meanings, connections, and the darkness of unanswered wonders. They lead people to creativity as well as critical insight. In many ways, the humanities fields structure the 'how' processes to produce the enduring 'why's' that drive new discovery, new clarity, and new contradictions. In fields like physics, chemistry, computer science, and biology, there is a specific goal in mind as their experiments continue. Even within sub-specialties, the focus on specialized techniques and conclusions drives the entire enterprise of scientific discovery. It is the rare moment when there is a breakthrough that challenges a fundamental question or assumption.

This approach to fundamental revision is the core of humanistic inquiry, especially since the transformation of the industrial imperial order between 1945 and 1975. Every form of human expression has confronted a crisis about the nature of human experience and knowledge. This process cannot be resolved quickly and neatly except through violence. Even in those cases, it only delays the inevitable conversations about what we know and why we know it. The inquiries in the humanities encourage the discovery of the range of falsehoods that human beings might encounter, and, more importantly, they craft the tools that people need to build the present and future truths that inspire new creativity.

The core of my 'why' -- based on both the pain I have inherited and the joy that I impart – is a shared purpose. It comes from an upbringing that combined the discipline of religious instruction with the praxis of **military** application. Those elements poured into a forge of civil and human rights activism to create an educator whose skills as a multimedia designer and as a historical researcher always strive for the highest standard of collaborative, interdependent excellence.

My 'why' is the common fire of humanity to create systems of justice, equity, **freedom,** and belonging. It is the beloved community empowered to create a world of beauty and dignity.

In the words of hip-hop poet Yasiin Bey,

Stop hidin'
Stop hidin'
Stop hidin' your face
because there ain't no hiding place

Our work together has the potential to reveal the grand design of human dignity if we can find the courage to stand together and face each other with integrity.

DR. WALTER GREASON

Dr. Walter D. Greason is the DeWitt Wallace Professor of History at Macalester College in Saint Paul, Minnesota. His research has defined new areas of inquiry in history, education, urban planning, and economics. Most known for his work on the concept of Wakanda as it appeared in Marvel Studios' film Black Panther, Dr. Greason uses advanced technology to transform schools and communities around the world.

Dr. Greason is an educator, a historian, an economist, and an urbanist all in one. For nearly 30 years, his unique interdisciplinary expertise and reach have connected millions of faculties, students, community leaders, and politicians to engage in global conversations about democracy, capitalism, and digital markets. These connections and conversations have sparked movements. They have initiated change. They have motivated people to act.

In addition to academic work, he is using his influence, expertise, and connections to act in supporting vulnerable communities. With support from strong relationships from academia and private sector partners alike, he focuses on using historic preservation as a means of reinvesting in vulnerable communities. The goal is to uplift communities by creating innovative ways to drive growth and opportunity and change policy, all while continually preserving the rich history and diversity of the area.

His work has inspired a revolution in social justice education over the last thirty years. Check out Walter's books and publications, including Suburban Erasure, Cities Imagined, Illmatic Consequences, Graphic History of Hip Hop #1, and much more, which are available on his website, Amazon, Academia, and most platforms.

Website: www.walterdgreason.com

Twitter (X): https://twitter.com/WalterDGreason

Instagram: https://www.instagram.com/walterdgreason

LinkedIn: wealthbuilder2050/

Facebook: DrWalterDavidGreason/

YouTube: https://www.youtube.com/user/wgreason/playlists

Rethinking Learning Podcast Episode #128:
Igniting Change through Global Conversations
https://bit.ly/episode128-greason

4

Near-Death-Experiences
That Changed My Life

DR. ILENE WINOKUR

*"Sometimes a little near-death experience
helps them put things into perspective."*
~ Anne Shropshire

Lately, there has been a lot of discussion about trauma's negative effect on mental health and a person's perspective, but I experienced an incident of trauma, a near-death experience (NDE), and it empowered me and gave me the courage to move out of my comfort zone. This story isn't meant to belittle those who've experienced trauma or traumatic experiences that still weigh heavily and cause pain or stress. This is one story that psychiatrists Tedeschi and Calhoun (2004) call post-traumatic growth.

These changes include improved relationships, new possibilities for one's life, a greater appreciation for life, a greater sense of personal strength, and spiritual development. There appears to be a basic paradox apprehended by trauma survivors who report these aspects of post-traumatic growth: Their losses have produced valuable gains.

You may be wondering, "How is this possible?" Let me start from the beginning ...

In March 2008, I was in Boston with my daughter to visit Babson College. She was interested in applying to the entrepreneurship major after she graduated from high school the following year. We wanted to take advantage of our free time and took a bus tour of the city's sights. The bus ended up near the wharf, so we decided to have lunch at Legal Seafoods, famous for its local lobster. After lunch, we took a walk since the weather was pleasant and the area was so beautiful. We walked through the Marriott Hotel to the pier where the boat tours originated. My daughter loves to take photos, so we stopped along the way for her to record our visit. At one point, there was a place where you could stand and look at the boats in the distance. The area is cordoned off by a low-slung black chain (about the height of my knee) that is strung across the length of the walkway. I stood a few inches in front of the chain with my back to the water and posed. My daughter positioned herself to take the photo and motioned for me to move a little to my left. She told me there was an ugly post next to me, and she didn't want it in the photo.

As I moved to the left, my shoe got caught in the groove between the concrete blocks on the sidewalk.

I lost my balance and began to fall backward over the chain. As I fell backward, I could see that there was nothing between me and the water ten feet below.

I could feel my purse sliding down my arm, and, for a brief moment, I pictured my money, credit cards, passports, and everything in my purse disappearing into the abyss below and ruining the rest of our trip.

Without thinking, I grabbed the purse's strap as it was about to leave my grasp. Almost simultaneously, I grabbed the black chain with my other hand, but my weight was still pushing me toward the edge of the walkway, and all I could think about was, 'I am going to drop headfirst into the cold, black water and that will be the end of me.'

Suddenly, I felt something, or someone, push at the back of my shoulder; in an instant, I was back on my feet. It was a surreal feeling since, moments before, my body was tumbling backward. Then I heard myself apologizing to all the people who rushed to help me: my daughter, a man pushing a baby stroller, and an older woman running faster than she should have been.

"I'm okay. Sorry for worrying you all," I called out.

My daughter rushed over to me, her face white as a sheet, and asked me if I was hurt. All I could feel was a bit of soreness on my hip where I had initially landed before jumping or being pushed back up, so I told her I was fine. I posed for the photo again and made sure this time to watch where I stepped. She snapped the picture, and we headed out, not saying another word about what had just happened.

We spent the afternoon walking around Boston and chatted about many things, but we didn't mention my near-death experience until later that evening while we were having dessert in a restaurant at the Prudential Center. While we were waiting for our order, I told my daughter that I had something I wanted to share with her about my "near accident" and asked if it was alright with her. I knew it had shaken her, and I didn't want to upset her if she wasn't ready to discuss it. She nodded her head that it was fine with me to talk about it. This is what I told her:

"It might seem strange, but it felt like someone pushed me or lifted me back on my feet while I was falling backward." Her facial expression completely changed as I spoke as she told me, "Mama, I wasn't going to say anything to you because I didn't want to upset you, but that's how it looked to me. It seemed like someone helped you get back up, but I knew nobody was there."

I could feel the goosebumps going up and down my arms. There was nothing else to say. We changed the subject and ate our delicious desserts, and that seemed to be the end of my near-death experience. But it wasn't.

I began to feel different. I thought about feeling like someone had pushed me back up as I was falling backward and that my daughter had "seen" it also. I believe in guardian angels and felt that MY guardian angel was looking after me that day. I felt grateful for being alive and blessed that I was able to share that spirituality with my daughter, even though it was initially traumatic for both of us. Researchers Shanna and Greyson note in their 2015 study.

To the extent that NDEs are interpreted by the experiencers as spiritual events, (our) findings support previous evidence that spiritual factors play a significant role in post-traumatic growth (Calhoun et al., 2000; Tedeschi and Calhoun, 1995; Werdel et al., 2014) (754).

The work of Shanna and Greyson underscores the role of spirituality when it "involves the search for meaning and purpose that may include transcendence (the experience of existence beyond the physical and psychological)" (749). In my case, I gradually felt a sense of empowerment and a new source of courage every time I thought about what happened that afternoon. I felt more confident and able to overcome the fear of failing.

The following year, I had another near-death experience. I was home alone on a Friday night, and the doorbell rang. I was upstairs watching television and answered through the intercom system. The male voice spoke Arabic, but I could tell it was not his native language. He said he had a delivery, and I told him that he must have the wrong address (which often happened due to the location of our house). I closed the intercom phone and went back to watching TV. About 10 minutes later, I heard a loud bang. It sounded like something had exploded, so I opened the door near the stairs and listened. Then I heard footsteps, and although I knew it couldn't be my husband because he was out with his friends, I shouted his name down the stairs. Almost immediately, two men, one with a kitchen knife in his hand, bolted up the stairs, two at a time. I screamed and tried to run, but the man with the knife grabbed the collar of my shirt and put the knife close to my neck.

"Shut up and stop screaming," he shouted at me as he moved the knife closer to my neck. "Where is your vault?" he screamed.

My life flashed by me as I tried to think of what to tell him. Unlike most other Kuwaiti families, we didn't keep our valuables in the house and rarely kept much cash. But I knew if

I told him that, he wouldn't believe me, and my life would be at risk. So, I stopped screaming and pointed to my bedroom. He pulled me to standing and pushed me toward the room as he motioned to his friend to start opening my jewelry box that was on top of my dresser and to open all the cabinets and drawers. I had just withdrawn cash from the bank because I was travelling the following week, and they found it in the shoebox where I kept it. They also found some gold jewelry I had been given when I got married in 1984.

As the accomplice rummaged through my dresser and the leader held onto my collar, I prayed they would leave without hurting me and avoid going to the TV room where I had left my cell phone. They were only in the house for about 10 minutes when it seemed they got nervous based on a call from the driver of their getaway car, which was evidently parked on the side of our house. After tying my hands behind my back with the wire from the bedroom lamp and threatening me not to tell anyone, they rushed downstairs. I waited for about five minutes (which seemed like hours) and then walked to the TV room, all the while trying to undo the knot in the wire. With my hands tied behind my back, I did my best to pick up my phone and call my husband. He didn't pick up, so I dialed the emergency number and did my best to explain that I'd just been robbed at knifepoint. They said they'd notify the police. Then my husband called, and I told him he needed to get home right away.

As I gently tiptoed downstairs, the doorbell rang. *'Who on earth could be ringing the doorbell?'* I thought. As I made my way toward the front door, I realized what the loud noise was. The thieves had taken the tire jack from their car and forced the wooden door open. Then I saw the helper from my brother-in-law's house at the door. She had been instructed to ring the doorbell because my husband thought the thieves were still inside the house and would leave if they thought someone was at the door. My in-laws were not at home, so they sent their helper.

One of my neighbors saw me sitting on the sofa in the living room (remember that the door was torn off its hinges) and asked if I was alright. By that time, I had been able to loosen the knot and free my hands. I guess my husband had called whoever he could think of might be nearby since it would take him twenty minutes to get home. When he arrived, he told me we had to go to the local police station to report the incident, which we did. Based on what I told them about the phone they used to call the driver, they were able to arrest them a few days later.

This incident shook me quite a bit. As I mentioned, I was set to travel soon after it happened, which turned out to be a good thing since I was able to distance myself from the memory of it and be around my family and friends in the U.S. In the meantime, I insisted that my husband install security cameras around the house before I returned so I could see who was at the door if I was upstairs when the doorbell rang.

When I returned to Kuwait a few months later, I was determined to move past what happened. I reminded myself that I had survived in 2008 because my guardian angel took care of me, and I survived the home robbery because my prayers were answered. My guardian angel was looking out for me again that night. It's important to note that "the researchers studying posttraumatic growth have been careful not to dismiss the pain of overcoming adversity" (Robson).

The change in my worldview didn't happen overnight. I felt anxious every time I recounted the robbery to those who asked me about it, and sometimes I had nightmares. But I wanted to continue living in my home, and I wasn't going to let anyone, or anything intimidate me.

I don't think about my near-death experiences often, but when I do, I feel a sense of power that I had never felt before. I survived two terrifying moments in my life, and that had to mean something. My life could be over in a second, so what did I want to do with it now? Who I was and what I wanted from life became clearer. That was my post-traumatic growth journey to figuring out my *why* and strengthening my sense of self belonging. In 2016, this feeling was within me when I met with my staff in response to an encrypted email sent to the university's management and my whole team by an unnamed and very disgruntled staff member. In my speech, I looked at each and every person in the room.

At age 59, I am aware of my strengths and faults. I don't need someone else to tell me who I am. I was given a mandate by the upper management and university board to make major changes to our curriculum and improve the toxic climate of our department...The train is on the tracks and moving forward. If anyone is unhappy with our direction, feel free to get off.

Near-death experiences are traumatic. How we view them as we sift through what happened can help us come out better on the other side. It comes down to how we view what happened in the context of our lives and especially how we want to live in the future.

Wondering

Do we become mired in what happened and let it bring us down, or do we come to terms with it (whether on our own or with the help of friends, family, or professionals) and let it guide us toward a better self-view and worldview?

References

Khanna, Surbhi, and Bruce Greyson. "NDEs and Posttraumatic Growth." The Journal of Nervous and Mental Disease vol. 203, no. 10, October 10th, 2015, pp. 749-755.

Robson, David. "The Complicated Truth of Post-traumatic Growth." March 14th, 2022, https://www.bbc.com/worklife/article/20220311-the-complicated-truth-of-post-traumatic-growth Tedeschi, Richard G., and Lawrence Calhoun.

"Posttraumatic Growth: A New Perspective on Psychotraumatology." vol. 21, no. 4, 2004.

DR. ILENE WINOKUR

Dr. Ilene Winokur is a professional development specialist with a focus on mentoring and coaching teachers globally, including refugee teachers. Ilene has been active in learning innovation for over 25 years and is passionate about narratives related to belonging. Prior to retiring in 2019, she was a teacher and administrator at the elementary and pre-college levels for 25 years, specializing in teaching English learners.

Ilene hosts a podcast and blogs about her personal journey to belonging in Buffalo, NY, where she grew up, and Yarmouk, Kuwait, where she has lived since 1984. Both focus on the importance of feeling a sense of belonging, the subject of her book, *Journey to Belonging: Pathways to Well-Being.*

41

A companion book with additional strategies and lesson ideas, *Finding Your* Pathway *to Belonging in Education,* was published in February 2023.

You can connect with Ilene on social media @IleneWinokur and find out more about one-to-one coaching, her asynchronous course on self-belonging, and links to her podcast and blog on her website: https://www.ilenewinokur.com

Podcast Episode #41 on Mentoring Teachers
https://bit.ly/episode41-winokur

Reflection #3 Belonging during this Pandemic:
https://bit.ly/reflection-ileneandbarbara

5

Write the Book

"Never let self-doubt hold you captive."
~ **Roy Bennett**

great source for connecting educators has been through
weekly online Twitter (X) chats. My deepest bonds
formed with people I connected with often in these chats.

My active participation online resulted in Shelley Burgess and
Beth Houf, authors of "Lead Like a Pirate" inviting me to guest-
host the #LeadLAP chat. I was honored and was excited to prep
weeks ahead of the date. The chat on Saturday, May 30, 2020.
Was during the early days of the COVID-19 pandemic,

In the States. education leaders were very concerned about
student learning loss. As the guest host, I led a conversation on
why educators should shift from using deficit language, such as
gaps, to filling buckets by focusing on the resilience of students,
parents, and teachers. Participants were given a question to
respond to as a "slow chat" throughout the following week.

Take another look at the date of the chat: May 30th, 2020. It
was mere days after George Floyd's murder. I was supposed to
facilitate conversations throughout the week on shifting
language and thinking. There was no way I could keep talking

about COVID related learning mindset and language when the world was hurting and so was George Floyd's family. I reached out to Beth and Shelley to tell them I couldn't continue the conversation as it was and asked if I could shift to what was in front of us.

They graciously gave their #LeadLAP Twitter space to the conversation of social justice, racism, antiracism, and equity. They were genuinely compassionate, supportive, and ready.

I facilitated conversations each week with superintendents, administrators, and educators. The conversations were carefully crafted to help individuals process on a personal level to begin to grasp the vastness and the depth of the pain of racism and how each of us can be part of the change. On a professional level, it was to help them lead with empathy in their educational spaces and with an awareness of the weight that many of their students and staff carry without knowing. It was time to begin to look through a different lens from an operational perspective and begin to analyze systems, processes, climate, and culture and plan for improvement and change. The conversations were based on questions that led participants to deeply challenge their thinking and to seek learning on their own.

This was hard. I was still processing my own emotions and navigating conversations how to support my family. There were protests, and the news was overflowing with outrage and reaction to George Floyd's murder. My mind played games with me. I am guiding superintendents and administrators, yet I don't have a degree in the subject.

Imposter syndrome would attempt to have me believe I was not enough. I was not qualified so I did some serious self-talk.

I have powerful prerequisites. I am Black. I am a woman. I am married to a Black man. I have two Black sons. I had to remind myself that I was more than qualified. So, I continued leading chat participants each week with Beth and Shelley as a profound source of support and strength. They were angry just like me. They wanted to help others with the resources they had available to them. Dave Burgess and Tara Martin of Dave Burgess Consulting, Inc. (DBC) were also extremely supportive of my commitment and passion for helping others and shared and curated the content from the chat each week.

Because Beth and Shelley were committed to these conversations for the foreseeable future, I knew the value of other Black voices coming alongside me to provide a variance of perspective and experience. With their once again unwavering support, I invited my friend, Dawn Harris to join me in taking #LeadLAP participants on a journey of what I called Leading by Learning. Working with Dawn exactly was what I prayed it would be...driven, passionate, and committed to making the world a better place. Together, for many months to come, we worked to bring participants to a better understanding of racism, bias, privilege, and the need to change, grow, transform, and be better human beings for ourselves and our students. Behind the scenes, we shared tears, stories, and emotions. The four of us grew tremendously as human beings and as friends committed to doing what we could to make the world a better place.

While this was happening, I was writing my first book with DBC, which was supposed to be about the joy of teaching. While leading educators through conversations, my own family was experiencing its own racially charged encounters. What I didn't realize was how much of my reality was being unintentionally woven into my manuscript. After submitting my manuscript, DBC came back to me and encouraged me to consider focusing primarily on the stories that had been unconsciously woven throughout the manuscript. They assured me that I guide and lead others with empathy and compassion and said the world needed more of this.

I had to sit with this for some time. The snippets to which they were referring to would involve elaboration on scenarios involving my sons, husband, and me. The mama bear in me did not want to put my family out into the universe. I sat with this some more, with so many thoughts swirling in my head that I finally shared this renewed information with my husband. His immediate response was total agreement. The next step was to talk to my sons. I spoke to each of them individually. Each one gave their full support and encouragement for me to "Write the book." These were the three words they spoke with boldness.

If I'm being completely honest, I was hoping they would not agree. I was hoping they said no. When they all consistently spoke the three words I will always remember, "Write the book," I knew I had to look in the mirror and own what I knew I was called to do.

When I began to write, I felt like I was going down a steep hill on a roller coaster. My stomach was in all kinds of knots as I mentally, visually, and emotionally relived each story I attempted to share in the book. I went through some things, but I reminded myself to lean into my faith. Self-talk also proved to be powerful source of encouragement to push through the emotions and continue writing. The more the voice of doubt spoke, the voice of courage overpowered.

Three years in the making, I can stand before you today and say I have completed the most challenging task of my life. I can also tell you it is a work of which I am in absolute awe. The beauty of the book lies in the heart of its purpose.

"Be the Change You Want to See" is crafted to foster deep, vulnerable, life, and heart-impacting conversations that will ultimately inspire all of us to be the change we want to see. Guiding readers through three phases, Listening, Learning, Being.

The first section asks readers to *listen* with their hearts as I share intimate, personal stories, and others ripped from the headlines. The second section guides readers through unpacking what they just read in the first section and owning their own *learning*.

In the third and final section, the state of *being*, I share the steps I have taken to make a difference and encourage readers to be the change they want to see. My hope is for conversations to abound because of reading the book conversations in homes, at work, in the community, places of worship, and organizations…will occur for people to listen to one another, to learn from one another, and to commit to being better human beings. For people who have been subjects of racism, bias, and discrimination, my hope is that there can be growth in sharing stories and move beyond the very real and legitimate "I shouldn't have to tell you, my feelings." Because to truly facilitate change, we must use our voices and share our stories.

My hope is in reading the book, conversations will abound in homes, at work, in the community, places of worship, and organizations. People will listen to one another, to learn from one another, and to commit to being better human beings. For people who have been subjects of racism, bias, and discrimination, my hope is that there can be growth in sharing stories and move beyond the very real and legitimate, "I shouldn't have to tell you feelings." To truly facilitate change, we must use our voices and share our stories.

I didn't *write the book* for me. I wrote the book to help make the world a better place. I also wrote it to show my sons that they can do the hard, impossible things. I wanted to show them what happens when someone believes in them – because they believed in me.

Wonderings

What's that one thing that you have stood at the base of the mountain dreaming about and looking up at the peak, thinking you'll never make it to the top? That thought process attempts to disguise itself, but let's call it out as what it is: fear and self-doubt.

- Identify your biggest dream, your most heartfelt passion, that thing that wakes you from your sleep.

- Identify your support team, meet with them, and ask them to go on the journey with you. Keep pushing yourself, and do not give up. DO. NOT. GIVE. UP.

Do you have something you are passionate about but let self-doubt and fear creep in, so you don't act on it? That imposter syndrome is real.

I believe this happens to many of us, especially when the challenge ahead of us seems unattainable.

You may feel you are not good enough, or you don't think you could do something you are passionate about. If you are passionate about that one thing and believe in yourself, you can do it. In fact, no one will be able to stop you if you believe that you can.

TRACI BROWDER

Traci Browder, M.Ed., is a trailblazer in education, inspiring and mentoring teachers and changing the lives of children for more than 20 years. Traci is known best for her innovative, out-of-the-box teaching style with a mixture of Montessori, gifted/talented, and special services all rolled into one classroom environment.

Traci possesses a Master's in Curriculum and Instruction from Dallas Baptist University and has experience as a classroom teacher, reading specialist, and instructional coach. Traci has an extensive marketing and communications background and uses all these skill sets as a consultant, author, and speaker.

Website: https://tracibrowder.com/
Podcast: Intelligogy The Podcast
Speaker Page:
https://www.daveburgessconsulting.com/speakers/tracibrowder/
Twitter(X): @tracibrowder | @intelligogy | @gritcrewedu
Instagram: @tracibrowder
Facebook: @tracibrowder & @tracibrowderMEd
Linkedin: @tracibrowder
YouTube: TraciBrowder

Rethinking Learning Podcast Episode #122:
Being an Advocate and Champion for Equity
https://bit.ly/episode122-browder

6

Spark

"Life is better when you're laughing."
~ Author Unknown

I t all started when I was in third grade when Mrs. Evans shared her spark of teaching and a different way of learning! Before I share that experience, let me scroll back to my childhood.

I grew up in south-eastern Ohio in the small town of Rutland. A rural community that had no traffic lights, one gas station, a department store, and a pizza place. I grew up LOVING sports! My two older brothers, Rob and John, were both active. I grew up watching them play baseball, basketball, and more! My parents taught us to never quit and always speak up for what we believe in!

My years in elementary school are kind of a blur. I do know I was average, but I needed lots of help with reading. I was pulled for extra reading help all through elementary school. In first grade, I had my own corner because I couldn't stop talking. I remember the archaic desks, which were placed in rows where I was given worksheets. It was a lot of 'sit and get' with the teacher at the front of the classroom talking and students quietly sitting.

Things changed in third grade when I had Mrs. Evans. She ignited a spark in me by showing me a new way to learn. It was where collaboration was born, and our voices were empowered. She was also creative, patient, and so much fun! From there, my SPARK was ignited.

My school years were filled with sports, especially playing softball, which I loved. I was an average student and excited about college. My dream was to attend the University of Rio Grande, majoring in elementary education and playing softball for the University. During my senior year in high school, I was offered a placement in an elementary school to observe a teacher. At that moment, I felt in my heart that was what I was meant to do.

Fast forward to college, when I was accepted into the education program at the University of Rio Grande and walked into the softball program, I was living my dream! My college years brought me so much happiness! I met so many amazing friends, played softball for college, hit a grand slam my freshman year, met my husband, and married him the year after we graduated. It was such a special time in my life.

My SPARK continued after graduating. I was excited to get a job. My WHY at that moment was to make a difference in a child's life. Of course, just like all graduates, I applied EVERYWHERE and had no luck. So, I substituted for about a year teaching grades K-8, which was quite the experience. After teaching as a substitute, I was so excited to get a job offer at an Islamic and Arabic school. I accepted the offer and learned so much from my first teaching job! I learned all about the

Islamic/Arabic culture and created the curriculum with my friend in Literacy, Math, Science, and Social Studies.

I again applied everywhere in the latter part of my first year at Sunrise Academy, which was an Islamic/Arabic school. I also created the curriculum with another teacher for the second graders. I learned so much about the culture and religion. After the year, I was elated to get a second-grade job at Avery Elementary in Hilliard City Schools, which was the district I was passionate about teaching in.

My WHY remained the same, and I was still very young and learning as much as I could. As the years progressed, I loved my profession even more. The kids were amazing, and I learned so much from them each year.

Fast forward to thirteen years later, I went for a routine mammogram. The doctors spotted a suspicious area and wanted to do a biopsy. During the biopsy, another spot was also suspicious. I was a little concerned, but I was young and had been checked regularly, so my odds were good on positive results.

Days later, I got the call that my biopsy was indeed cancer.

It took a while to process, but my initial reaction was, "Cancer messed with the wrong chick!"

I was determined to BEAT it: to watch my girls grow up, their graduation, marriage, have kids, and be a grandma. There was SO much more living I needed to do!

I remember meeting with the surgeon to plan my treatment. He had appointments free in August, but I asked to wait until late September so I could meet my second-grade family. He was okay with that, and I had some normalcy before my big procedure.

I remember that my kids were both the best distraction and medicine. I had a lumpectomy and radiation, which meant I was off for about a month. Even though I was going through all of that, I used Flipgrid, which is now called Microsoft Flip, to engage with my kiddos, discuss how the days went, new info, or just say hi! I needed to keep the lines of communication open.

My kids continue to be my WHY even during the rocky times. Their SPARK ignites my SPARK :)

The roller coaster continued. As I started radiation, they found a lump in my thyroid. I was referred to an endocrinologist who recommended surgery. I kept putting it off and finally agreed when they did find that it was thyroid cancer.

A year later, doctors found precancerous cells in my cervix and highly recommended a hysterectomy, which I had. During all of these hiccups: breast cancer, thyroid cancer, and a hysterectomy, my faith has never been stronger. My passion, my SPARK, and my WHY have never faded or waivered. I could not have done it without my amazing family: both my second-grade family and my personal family, as well as friends and colleagues!

In the school year of 2019/2020, I was told I would be transferring to another school. I was reluctant as I had been with this school for over 20 years. I had created relationships with not only my kids but also parents, community, and staff. Yet, I was excited for a new adventure. Then Covid hit, and I was told they needed me online.

Online!?! I had no idea what to expect. I consistently kept hearing, "You'll be awesome!" "You're so great with tech!" My mind didn't go to technology. It went to my kids and how I was going to establish relationships. The following questions kept me thinking about my situation.

- Am I doing enough?
- How will I show my love for my students over a screen?
- How will I do all the interactive activities online?

To say I was apprehensive is an understatement! I can honestly say that I had NO idea what I was getting myself into. I was apprehensive, nervous, and knew no one. There was a total of ten second-grade teachers that year, each with a class size close to 30. It was a HUGE adjustment, and I learned what the words 'adjust and adapt' really meant!

That year, my mental health was challenged, also my confidence, but I learned so much about myself. I learned that no matter the medium of learning, my kids were going to have fun, make memories, spread kindness, and build relationships. During that year, we mystery zoomed with every state, had a genius hour, had student-led conferences, played hide and seek in Zoom, had dance parties, and SO MUCH MORE. I learned so much about myself that year. I learned that ...

(1) Grace is necessary.

(2) Patience and flexibility are a must.

(3) Laugh often, and so much more!

I enjoyed the adventure and was blessed to have amazing kids and parents! It made me grow as an educator and person!

Fast forward to 2023-2024, and it's my third year in my new school! I absolutely LOVE the kids, parents, and staff! My SPARK continues to grow and glow! Now I can say I am so blessed to have the opportunity to ignite a SPARK in my kids like Mrs. Evans did with me!

Have you found your SPARK?

MELISA HAYES

Melisa Hayes is currently a second-grade teacher. She has a bachelor's and a master's degree in education. This will be her 27th year in education. Melisa is a Wakelet, Flip, & Night Zookeeper ambassador, Teach Better ambassador and an Apple Distinguished Educator. She was awarded as a Distinguished Educator in her district four years ago and was awarded Global Teacher of the Year three years ago.

Melisa is a part of Our Global Classroom, which is a family of educators around the globe who always put kids first. They strive to teach the UN Sustainable Development Goals (SDGs) and bring a universal call to action to better our world! She is passionate about many things: inclusion, teaching the whole child, establishing relationships with my kids, and creating a FUN, safe environment where her kids have a voice and choices and are empowered daily!

In her free time, Melisa loves to spend time with her family: her husband and two girls, Maddy and Abby. They love walking their dog, board games, travelling, and making memories. She also loves being active: playing softball, walking, biking, or running.

Melisa is a LIFELONG learner. She loves learning new and innovative ways to engage her kids and staying connected to her Professional Learning Family on Twitter as @MrsHayesFam and Voxer. They continue to motivate and inspire Melisa daily! Melisa's children's book, "A B B S" launched in Fall 2023.

Twitter (X) @MrsHayesfam

Facebook: melisa.hayes.925

Instagram: melisa.6782

Rethinking Learning Podcast Episode #138: Engaging Inclusive Environments While Empowering Learners
https://bit.ly/episode138-hayes

7

Drawing My Purpose

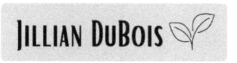

"How you draw reflects how you feel about the world.
You're not capturing it; you're interpreting it."
~ Juliette Aristides

I vividly remember the feeling of my pencil on paper as a young child learning to draw. The sensation stirred up emotions in me as I brought lines, squiggles, and shapes to life. It was as if I had found a secret way to capture a moment in time and preserve it forever in my memory. While I didn't comprehend it at the time, I could spend hours lost in my own world, creating my own ideas, without a care in the world.

As my life story unfolded, I came to realize that drawing was my way of expressing myself and connecting with others. Through my artwork, I could share my unique experiences and perspectives with the world. I learned to communicate my joy, my sorrow, my hopes, and my dreams. Eventually, I became aware of how to see the world in a new way.

My Aunt Casey was a brilliant artist, and her skill with watercolors always amazed me. I wanted to follow in her footsteps, so she took me to my first art lessons when I was ten years old. I was wide-eyed and open to taking in all of the creativity that I could. I quickly fell in love with the process of art. I loved seeing the palettes of colors, understanding the visual perspectives, and finding my own style of expression. I felt like I could create anything I could imagine.

My first drawings/illustrations when I was 10.

As the years went on, I continued to explore the world of art. I found beauty in the works of many different artists, but I was particularly drawn to the Impressionists. I loved the way they subtly depicted the beauty of the natural world in their paintings. I related to my favorites like Monet, Cassatt, Degas, and Sisley, who often painted outdoors rather than in a studio. As Sisley once said, "Every picture shows a spot with which the artist has fallen in love." (Sisley) They captured the beauty of these places in their paintings, and in doing so, they shared their love with the world. I admired the movement and texture that occurred in their soothing and calming patterns. This hobby was more than just recreation for me. It became a place where I could find tranquility and peace.

I enjoyed designing drawings for others, often giving my works as gifts to friends and family. The types of drawings I created varied depending on the recipient's interests. For example, I would often paint houses, landscapes, or lighthouses.

When painting a house, I would carefully choose the right specifics, such as the shape of the roof, the color of the siding, and the details of the windows and doors. I would also try to capture the atmosphere of the house, whether it was a cozy cottage or a grand mansion.

The true reward of any act of giving is not in what you receive but in the happiness you bring to others.

Journaling the Journey

The COVID-19 pandemic brought about a lot of chaos and confusion. However, it also presented an opportunity for rest. For me, confinement brought about a sense of freedom. As an educator, I was able to teach virtually from home and create interactive activities for my students. I enjoyed the stillness. I am an introvert, so I was delighted with canceled plans, family dinners at home, and watching TV shows.

At first, I enjoyed the peace and quiet of the pandemic, but it soon became mundane. I was looking for a new source of contentment, and that's when I discovered my purpose.

I started to reflect on my life's journey and thought about all the difficulties and disappointments I had faced. I recalled the heartache of infertility as my husband, and I tried to conceive for years. We called this our "valley" as we walked through those dark days of barrenness. But through the struggle, we found hope through adoption. Our son, Austin, was the greatest gift we could ever have imagined.

I thought about other letdowns in my life. I had lost several family members to a rare genetic cancer. It was a devastating blow to our close-knit family. My cousin, uncle, father, and sister all died from the disease within a few years of each other. The grief was intense. I felt physically exhausted, and I had trouble sleeping. I also had headaches and stomach aches. Mentally, I was overwhelmed with sorrow, anger, and confusion. It took me a long time to process my grief. Talking to others who understood what I was going through helped me to feel less alone.

I didn't want to relive the traumatic memories, but they gave me an opening to start working through my grief. I decided to start journaling and sketching out my feelings. There were no right or wrong answers, and I didn't have to follow any rules. I needed to be honest and vulnerable with myself. No one else would see what I wrote or drew. This was my creative outlet.

Soon, I started adding my sketches and notes to my iPad. This was a much simpler way to keep everything together digitally. I found an app called Procreate, which was a powerful and intuitive tool. It was like having a magical art studio right in my lap. There were thousands of brushstrokes, palettes, textures, and medium choices. I was able to express my grief in a new way. I could use the different tools to create images that represented my feelings. It was a cathartic experience. I felt like I was finally able to process my grief and start to heal.

My WHY IS Defined

I remember the day when the grief started to lift. I couldn't pinpoint the exact moment, but I knew that I had finally come out on the other side of mourning into a beautiful realization that the pain was lighter. I could take deliberate steps toward healing, and I felt a sense of peace and joy that I hadn't felt in a long time.

I think the greatest catalyst for my healing was writing about my emotions. I started a blog, then a manuscript for a children's book, and as I wrote, I was able to process my grief and connect with my purpose. I realized that we grieve because we love and that we remember because we STILL love. Even as we move into the understanding of the void, we can still recall the treasured memories, the laughs, the challenges, and the brokenness.

I fell in love with the story and pitched it to my Aunt Casey, asking for her advice. She enthusiastically took the initiative to help me craft the character, and we discussed the visual setting with creativity. After a few of our collaborative sessions, I asked her if she would consider illustrating the book, feeling confident that she would accept my offer. However, my hopes were dashed when she immediately turned me down only because she was certain that I could do it on my own.

She was right. I had never felt more ready to take on a challenge in my whole life. I was excited to bring the story into a reality, and I knew that I would do my best to make it something special.

After finishing writing *Liv's Seashells*, I began to tangibly draw the story. I poured my heart and soul into each illustration. The sandy beach, the unusual seashells, and the sparkling sun all seemed to leap off the page. As I edited the manuscript, the small yet mighty character came to life exactly as I had envisioned. I felt my sister's presence over my shoulder, her love and affection for the project evident in her quiet whispers.

I reviewed the pages ever so carefully. The pictures were a silent narrative, each one a scene that played out in my mind's eye. The details were so rich, and the emotions so palpable that I felt like I was right there, living the story along with young Liv. A small firefly on each page was a visual and heartfelt reminder that Lisa's spirit was always with me, lighting up even the darkest of spaces.

The pieces of the puzzle slowly came together, fitting perfectly like a mosaic. The colors, textures, and details were carefully chosen to create a sense of harmony and balance. The images were not random or chaotic, but rather, they were carefully arranged to create a meaningful journey. It was complete. A creative endeavor that was to be shared as a gift.

My sister Lisa was the inspiration, and I wrote it to honor her memory. She was my Liv in real life. Lisa was compassionate and empathetic. She saw the good in everyone, especially those who were different, broken, or imperfect. She welcomed them into her life with open arms, as if they were the most precious seashells she had ever found. The beach was one of her happy places, where she would search for the perfect sandy spot to soak up the splendid waves and salty air.

I knew how important it was to share the story of my sister's life with her daughter and son, who were very young when she died. My heart was set to tell them about her kindness, her compassion, and her exuberant love of life. I wanted to make sure they knew how special their mother was and that her love would always be in their hearts. She left them a legacy of faith and loyalty, which they could continue to build on.

Our souls have an amazing capacity to hold everything we need. There is room in **our** hearts to carry forward heartache and joy together. We can **embrace** the peaceable satisfaction and contentment that we have earned. And one glorious day, we find that the joy triumphs over the grief.

I am grateful for this journey I have been travelling and believe it has given me **strength**. I have learned that grief is a process and that it is okay to feel a range of emotions, including sadness, anger, and even joy. Joy is possible, even in the midst of pain. It is an outward expression of the marriage of contentment and heartache. These two emotions are not mutually exclusive, and they can coexist in our hearts.

The memories that flow from Liv's pages are a precious treasure and have provided a steady foundation for my WHY. I share her story with **others, especially** those who are struggling, because it contains messages of hope and resilience that we all need to hear.

Just keep writing, **keep talking**, and keep loving.
The joy will **come**.

Work Cited:

Sisley, Alfred. *"Alfred Sisley Quotes | Famous Quotations About Art & Artists."* ATX Fine Arts, https://www.atxfinearts.com/blogs/news/alfred-sisley-quotes. Accessed June 10th, 2023.

Lisa & me on the beach in our happy spot.

Liv from *Liv's Seashells*

JILLIAN DuBOIS

Jillian DuBois is a redesigned educator who has been in the elementary classroom for **over** 20 years. She is currently a Professional Learning Specialist with Forward Edge/Edge•U. Jill is passionate about infusing joy in educational leadership by focusing on service and using her voice to foster hope by celebrating diversity.

She is a published author and illustrator of several children's books with social-emotional learning messages. She is also the Chief Optimistic Originator of Imparted Joy LLC in Clearwater,

Florida. In this role, Jill guides others to spark their stories with heart and confidence.

Jillian is a dynamic **and** inspiring leader who is committed to making a difference in the lives of children and educators. She is a role model for educators everywhere, and her work is helping to create a more joyful and hopeful world for all.

LinkTr.ee: https://linktr.ee/jilliandubois

Rethinking Learning Reflection #13:
Choose and Impart Joy in Uncertain Times
https://bit.ly/reflection13-DuBois

Section 2

Journey Your Why

What story challenged you to choose another path on your journey to your why?

Each story from the contributing authors in this section is about something that surprised them along their journey. Something happened that might have changed the path they were going down. The challenge, struggle, or experience helped them realize the process they went through to redefine their purpose.

> *"If it doesn't challenge you,*
> *it won't change you."*
> **~ Fred DeVito**

Grow Your Why

8

Always Wanted to be a Teacher, But Didn't Want to Always be a Teacher

RICH SIMPSON

"Failure is an opportunity to begin again more intelligently."
~ **Henry Ford**

I come from a family steeped in army history and distinguished careers: Dad, Grandad, Great-Grandad, uncles, cousins—all military. So, no surprises; that was my plan, too. I had been dreaming about it, talking about it, reading books about it (of course). It was all laid out…get A-levels, go to university, then Sandhurst for officer training, four or more years' service, then out and on with civilian life after that (as a teacher).

All was going to plan: I got into university, did my 4-year teacher training degree, and then my NQT (Newly Qualified Teacher) year here on the Isle of Wight. I had been clear with my headteacher from the start -this was a one-year gig to get my NQT qualification before the Army, then maybe a return to teaching later in life. I had attended the selection week in Wiltshire and done the interviews and physicals, and she had been brilliant at letting me take time to do these and stay on a rolling contract until I had a definite intake date.

But...

"One last game for the team..." and that was it. Plan derailed: shoulder dislocated in a rugby match. I carried on at school for another year whilst I had physio and eventually three operations to sort out the damage, then returned to the plan! After more interviews, another selection event in the Spring term, and I got the nod: I had a place and date. January. The plan was back on track.

Except...

Life had happened. I'd bought a flat. I'd made friends. I enjoyed teaching. I had a girlfriend, and I was reconsidering everything ever so slightly.

But...THE PLAN! I'd had it so long it was all I could see and all I thought I wanted, so I carried on. I sold the flat, resigned from school, and dumped the girlfriend. Come December, I had cut all ties, ready to start the next stage, when the postman dropped a letter through the door. Army crest on the front... "Probably a list of things to do/bring/not bring!" I think. But I was not expecting them to tell me not to bother turning up at all!

That was not the plan! However, it's what happened, and as they say...best-laid plans and all that!

The shoulder had (literally, physically, and now career-wise, too) been a sticking point. The background medical checks before I turned up had flagged it up, and despite it not having been a problem on the physical tests in person themselves, on paper, it was a failure—before I'd even started.

So, what... I hear you say!

Life had been okay—I've already said that: friends, an ex-girlfriend who might forgive me, and I was enjoying teaching—just go back to that. The problem was, I'd be going back without having been anywhere. In my head, I'd left. I was going to do something different, and teaching was something I would return to later in life – the safe option after the service and adventure I'd hoped the Army might provide. So, I couldn't just carry on. I saw myself as a complete failure. The plan I'd shared with family and friends had not worked out, and I didn't know what to do and didn't want to face them having not done it.

I did leave. I left everything, and with no definite destination in mind, I went travelling. My mum has since admitted that she didn't think I'd ever come back. I wasn't sure exactly where I was going, so I'm not sure if I was going to either if I'm honest, but that's a dark road I don't want to go down.

What did I do?

After a few weeks licking my wounds and living in a friend's spare room, I packed up and disappeared. And it was one of the best things that had ever happened to me. 'THE PLAN' had been so rigidly set in my mind that I had neglected other things. Sure, I'd had fun – been on holidays with friends and family, but I had done nothing else other than summer jobs and university, then gone straight into teaching. So I took a year 'out'. It's now laughingly referred to as my "early mid-life crisis", but it was far from a crisis. It was cathartic.

I:

- Worked as crew for a month on a multi-million-pound super-yacht owned by a banker in London, who wanted it sailed around the Med so he could fly in for the odd weekend.

- I worked as a TEFL teacher in Bond Street in London.
- Went to lots of concerts (Foo Fighters 2 weeks in a row, anyone?).
- Lived at a fight school in Thailand, trained for 3 hours a day in Muay Thai for three months (I have never been so fit!), and sparred with a world champion.
- Qualified as a PADI 'Rescue Diver' and nearly died after getting stuck in a shipwreck.

And I decided I wanted to be a teacher again…

I had gotten over the idea that I was only doing it because it was all that was left and was now going back to it because it was a job I *wanted* to do.

I was fortunate. I'd returned to the island for the music festival, and having met up with some old friends, I heard that my old school needed maternity leave cover. I applied and was soon back in familiar territory with friends, a school I knew, and a job I realized I loved.

I took the desire to lead and turned it to teaching, starting my Aspiring Middle Leaders course, and becoming Lower

School leader and English coordinator. I found a passion for teaching that previously hadn't been there, enhanced by the experiences I had gained during my year away.

This chapter wasn't supposed to be an autobiography: there is a more profound and more general point, and that is this: plans are great, but "What if...?" Success is great, but failure happens, often more so than success on life's journeys.

I could have let the failure drag me down into depression and despair (and those were there at times, I admit), but if that happened every time, we didn't get our way, life would be pretty grim, and it's not! Life is great—full of countless opportunities, not just the one you have your heart set on. Yes, it's good to have a focus and desire, but don't be blind to other possibilities! The activities and experiences I were fortunate enough to be able to do that year. It shaped me and stayed with me now. They've made me better as a person and as a teacher: more experienced, more rounded, more worldly-wise, certainly! And the joyous part—I can share those experiences with my pupils and show them that failure can be a starting point rather than an end...that "opportunity to begin again, more intelligently."

My big failure *was* a big one—a life decision/path that had to be completely reassessed, but that's not to say that this approach can't be filtered down to those everyday events that don't go to plan. If something doesn't work, then change it.

Move on...try something else...try again after a while or walk away completely! You might find that that moment of failure has opened a door or shown you a new way of looking at things that an easy success would never have let you have. The "intelligent" part comes not from doing the same thing again more cleverly but with more realization and the ability to choose what happens going forward.

Whilst I regret that my 'plan' didn't work out, I look back now afresh and without the raw emotion of the time. I would love to have served, as many of my family did (and my brother, who I'm immensely proud of, still does).

But.... I am extremely proud to say I've always been a teacher and ALWAYS will be.

Hold on!

Update! Life still isn't going to plan!

Life has moved on again since I wrote this chapter, and yet again, it is not as expected or desired!

My marriage of ten years broke down in October 2021 (just as my career was going well!), and I am now divorced and sharing custody of my two fabulous kids with my ex-wife. Not the way things are supposed to go, but it is another example of life throwing challenges at you. This one is still an ongoing one, as we all get used to different ways of being a family and doing the best for the children, as well as moving on with life.

In work, things have also moved on, and again, in an unexpected way...I completed my headteacher qualification here in the UK (it's called the "National Professional

Qualification for Headship)" and successfully applied for a Deputy job in a larger school. Shortly after that—talk about being thrown in at the deep end—we got an Ofsted inspection, where the school was upgraded to "Good".

On the back of that success, my headteacher was asked to support another school, and so I was asked to be head of my new school in an unexpectedly fast promotion, as well as working in collaboration with this other 'partner' school. I ended up teaching one day a week there, as well as then coming back and trying to run my own school - it's been a busy year and a very steep learning curve, which still doesn't look like it's slowing down! Safeguarding, staffing, and working with other schools—all great opportunities that I'm truly thankful for and that have enabled me to meet and work with even more fantastic educators.

I've loved the challenge, though, and the different roles I'm now having to take on are expanding my skills and experience in ways I'd never have thought would happen and in ways that would never have happened if I'd stayed as a classroom teacher. I do love being in front of a class of children, reading a story, and talking about new ideas, and if I'm honest, there are days when I wish that was still my full-time role. However, I'm pleased with the belief that has been shown in me and the trust placed in me to be able to facilitate great learning and run a school where learners get to have other great teachers in front of them because of the work I do!

To finish and look back on what I first wrote...the ALWAYS BE A TEACHER part of my original piece still stands. I'm working on remembering the purpose of a school and my place in it and focusing on meeting life's new challenges head-on.

Also, I am not expecting things to go to plan!

RICH SIMPSON

Growing up in Northern Ireland, **Rich Simpson** was part of a single-parent family, living with his younger brother, sister, and mum. His dad left when he was six or seven, and rarely saw him again after that. Life was tricky, possibly due to the unrest at home. Rich was not a happy child and didn't enjoy early school apart from books. He was excluded from pre-school and only allowed into primary school if medicated. Rich had few friends and was subjected to horrific bullying as an 'outsider' at a large all-boys secondary school.

A teacher called Mrs. Riddle spoke to his mum and persuaded her to let him try books as an alternative, and it changed everything.

Rich is now Acting Head of School in the Isle of Wight in the UK after being a Literacy Lead and Year 6 teacher. As a lifelong lover of books, Rich feels incredibly lucky to have been a teacher and passed the love of books on to others. He started "What I Read" as a way of sharing his love of books with an even wider audience. He blogs about books on his website https://www.whatiread.co.uk/ and spreads kindness with his handle **@richreadalot** and the hashtag **#kindnessripple** on Twitter (X).

Rethinking Learning Podcast Episode #112:
Spread the Kindness Ripple through Books
https://bit.ly/episode112-richsimpson

9

Generations of Family Trauma

NICOLE BISCOTTI

Exodus 34:7 - *Keeping mercy for thousands, forgiving
iniquity, transgression and sin, and that will by no means
clear the guilty; visiting the iniquity of the fathers upon
the children, and upon the children's children, unto the
third and to the fourth generation."*

I can remember the vein bulging on the pastor's forehead
and his voice rising as he pointed his finger, exclaiming that
the sins of the father were visited on to the children and their
children's children. I did not understand everything the pastor
was saying that day, but the way he moved around the stage in
front of the church with sweat pouring from his brow before
returning to the pulpit and clenching the bible in emphasis as he
spoke both captivated my eleven-year-old self's attention and
perplexed me.

Until that point, I had been taught that God was love, that
he was just. How could a God who loved me and was fair and
kind make me pay for sins that were committed by other people,
even if they were related to me? Everything in my body resisted
the idea of not having control over my own destiny, a reaction
that I have felt many times during my life and can trace back to
that very moment.

As the years went on, I began to understand that it was not God's fault that we have generational curses; it was simply a result of the patterns that families create. We either tend to repeat or refute what we lived as children. In both cases, we usually react without even realizing it rather than choosing our lives and living fully and purposefully.

Since I was a child, I have been very uncomfortable with the idea of *not* being able to do something that was important to me to accomplish. It feels stifling and as if life is monotonous without the freedom to pursue my goals and passions. When I originally went to college after high school, I quickly dropped out. I did not have the support or guidance to complete my education, and that unfulfilled dream left me feeling empty and disempowered.

Then, at the age of twenty-six and a single mother of a three-year-old, I mustered the courage to take an entrance exam at the college of my dreams. I became discouraged and did not finish the application process, so I was shocked to receive an acceptance letter. I was raised with very traditional views and was quickly told that I had absolutely no business pursuing a college degree when I had a son to take care of. It was pointed out that I would be taking time away from my son to attend college and study. To the reader, this might understandably sound absurd, but conditioning is powerful, and at that point, what I was hearing echoed only what I had been taught to believe. I loved my son wholeheartedly and desperately wanted to be a good mother. Therefore, I began to resign myself to the idea that I couldn't pursue higher education.

Harlem

by Langston Hughes
(my mother's favorite poem)

What happens to a dream deferred?

> *Does it dry up*
> *like a raisin in the sun?*
> *Or fester like a sore—*
> *And then run?*
> *Does it stink like rotten meat?*
> *Or crust and sugar over—*
> *like a syrupy sweet?*
> *Maybe it just sags*
> *like a heavy load.*
> *Or does it explode?*

My maternal grandmother, who we call Mama Mia, prides herself on living a very full life despite several disadvantages. She came from poverty, grew up in an orphanage (although her parents were alive), her parents were alcoholics, and the list goes on. She lives life on her terms, with confidence in her instincts, and refuses to be anything but the master of her own destiny. Mama Mia always says that the only regret she has in her life is that she never completed her education because she doesn't know what she could have become.

"For when a child is born, the mother also is born again."
~ Gilbert Parker

I woke up the next morning to a call from Mama Mia. She is both an early riser and has a commanding presence, so it was early in the morning, and she got straight to the point. She told me that during the night, she had a dream where my recently deceased grandfather spoke to her. He told her that the condo she had was large enough for her to have my son and me come live with her. This was a way that I could attend school and not have to work full-time. He told her that was his wish for their home. He said he knew it would make her happy to use that additional space to help me finish college because I was a "smart cookie".

By the time I was even awake enough to understand what Mama Mia was talking about, she was already explaining how she agreed with Papa because neither she nor Papa had ever finished their education and that it was time to turn things around in this family. My mother had recently completed her education as an adult, and now they wanted to help me. I'm not sure what the ramifications of talking to someone who is deceased in your dream are, but I can say with certainty that I had not discussed my aspirations of going back to school with Mama Mia. I knew that I needed to seize this opportunity.

It took me a long time, but I earned not only a bachelor's degree but two master's degrees and part of a doctoral degree. Pursuing my education began as checking off an unfulfilled goal. Along the way, I realized that education stretches your perspective and empowers you, opens doors, and increases your confidence in yourself. Initially, I had been neutralized from pursuing my dreams by the notion that I could not do so as a mother. As I continued along my educational journey, I began to realize that persevering to pursue my education had a profound effect not only on my ability to provide for my children but on their own futures as well.

We owe it to those who paved the way for us to see them and to acknowledge their limitations and their triumphs. Ultimately, the source of their strength was a vision larger than themselves - it was their hope for us. Their struggles were fought so that we could thrive, and their courage is our birthright. We carry prior generations in our DNA; they not only raise us but are the very essence of who we are genetically. We are conditioned by their values and imprinted with their hopes, dreams, and expectations of us. We must first understand their struggles and their courage before we can choose our own.

I now understand that generational trauma does not prevent us from our purpose but rather prepares us. The regrets my grandparents carried, and their stories of unfulfilled dreams instilled in me the importance of personal fulfillment. Watching my mother struggle to complete her education as a single mother provided a roadmap of how to accomplish the same for myself. Even the trauma that I suffered prepared me for my purpose. I have an innate empathy that serves my students.

I became an educator because I believe wholeheartedly in the personal transformation that education brings and the opportunities that it gives students. I also believe that *every* individual should have access to a quality education. For me, this is work that matters. This is work that is important because without it, others are not able to reach their potential, and as my grandmother stated, they don't even know who they can become.

We have a lot of work to do in education. We have become affected by polarized politics and a divisive society. My grandparents did not have the opportunity to have an education, but they understood the empowerment that it brings. We can't continue to offer that opportunity for upward mobility and development until we begin to respect and meaningfully include people from all walks of life and to equitably provide them with the support they need as well.

This is where my WHY, my purpose lies. Every child deserves to SHINE at school.

Beauty is in the eye of the beholder, and where others might see obstacles, I choose to see a perfect plan. When I uplift a child, I am also raising my voice, that of my grandmother and all of those who came before me and led me to where I am today.

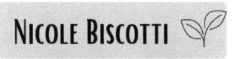

Nicole Biscotti is a Momvocate, Educator, and author whose focus is on the future of school as being informed by relevancy and the needs of our currently marginalized, under-supported learners.

We have a lot to learn if we listen!

Nicole wrote *I Can Learn When I'm Moving: Going to School With ADHD* http://bit.ly/icanlearnwhenimove with her nine-year-old son from the unique perspectives of a child and a mother who is also a teacher. She empowers parents and teachers to provide game-changing support for children with ADHD in school by sharing her and her son's story, along with research-based strategies.

Nicole has also translated books into Spanish such as El Cuento del Perdón by Melody McAllister and Todos Pueden Aprender Matemáticas by Alice Aspinall. I Can Learn When I'm Moving is also coming soon en español.

Her next book, co-authored with Dr. Tracy Scott Kelly, *Invisible Con ADHD:* Real *Voices, Real Policy for Latino Students,* addresses the issues around the disproportionate lack of support that Latino children with ADHD face. Nicole is co-host of a podcast: "Real Talk with Barbara and Nicole," about authenticity in a polarized society. #RealTalkBN

You can connect with Nicole at NicoleBiscotti.com/

Twitter (X) @BiscottiNicole, **IG:** @MeaningfulInclusionEdu or join her **Facebook group** #ADHDGlobalConvo
Real Talk Podcast: realtalkbn.buzzsprout.com

Rethinking Learning Podcast Episode #85: Writing to Uplift, Inform, and Bridge Understanding
https://bit.ly/episode85-biscotti

Podcast Reflection #14: Why I Can Learn When I'm Moving with Nicole Biscotti and her son, Jason
https://bit.ly/reflection14-Biscotti

10

Learning from My Journey (as a recurring One Black Friend)

HEDREICH NICHOLS

"I did then what I knew how to do.
Now that I know better, I do better."
~ Maya Angelou

If you've heard SmallBites or been in one of my keynotes or sessions, you may have heard my story about wanting a Confederate flag for my room when I was a teenager. If not, here goes:

I was riding in the car with my mom and Big Cyp, our church organist. We pulled up to a light next to a big Ford truck, decked out, as was common in the 80s, with big tires, a big gun rack, and a giant rebel flag in the back window.

"Oooh, y'all look," I gleefully exclaimed. "I want one of those!"

"One of what?"

"One of those flags," I continued, excitedly pointing to 'Old Dixie', the hallmark of Southern pride I had been taught about growing up in the Texas school system.

"Hedreich, do you know what that is?!"

At that moment, long before the word 'gaslighting' was a thing, I knew I had been duped, deluded, and manipulated into believing in the South and the Southern symbols of oppression as noble and worthy of my affection.

I was a senior in high school, and before that moment, I had never questioned the celebration of a war that, had it been won by the South, would have had me in the cotton fields still. Until that moment, it never really occurred to me that while we all went to school together, we mostly went home to segregated neighborhoods and churches. It didn't dawn on me that of all my mom's friends, not one of them was White, and of all my friends in twelve years of being in schools with were mostly white people. I had never been to a birthday party at their homes, nor had they come to mine. At that moment, I realized that there was something missing, an elephant in the room that was never discussed. That moment was the beginning of my journey.

My journey continued later that year. I went on to college in North Carolina, where, in my very first class, the girl behind me tapped me on the shoulder and said, "I never met a colored before." I was shocked. One that she'd never met anyone other than whites, and two, that she used the word 'Colored'—in the 80s! As I slowly realized that *North* Carolina was still very much the South, little things kept the journey alive. For example, I also realized that the university had asked for pictures of our housing applications because they wanted to pair Blacks with Blacks and Whites with Whites in dorms. After all, if we hadn't been to each other's birthday parties or even known folks of other 'races', we certainly could not be expected to share rooms. And then, there was the nice White guy who took me to a nice restaurant where the hostess looked at each of us twice before asking, "*Two* for dinner?"

It seemed that after seeing—really seeing—the Confederate flag, I saw things more clearly, something that I had been conditioned not to notice. In my Communications 101 class, I remember learning about code-switching. It was there that I began to see my life's dance between two worlds through an academic lens. It was then that I began to understand the energy expended perfecting that dance. It is only recently that I understand and grieve that energy as needlessly lost. What if I had not known, in the back of my head, that I wasn't like 'them'? What if I had not had to learn and perfect the codes of power in white settings and instead had been able to use that energy to organize, study, write, create, and achieve?

You always wonder about the road not taken, and I do sometimes wonder what my life would have been like had I been born in a place where the people in stations of political power and wealth all looked like me. I know Black people like that, people from Jamaica or Eritrea or Nigeria. They have a sense of confidence that I can only keep pressing towards. But overall, even growing up in a time when almost nobody on TV or in magazines looked like me, I've fared well. As I state in my book *Finding Your Blind Spots*, I was a 'credit to my race,' the affable black girl who skipped a grade and could sing. I was well-behaved, 'well spoken,' and had all the 'codes of power' a Black person needed to be successful in a White world. Still, what if, instead of learning to code-switch masterfully, I'd have had that cognitive energy for academic pursuits? Would I have been a better college student my first time around? Would I have finished the books I started in the 90s? Would I have been a better teacher, parent, or even friend?

> *"The need for change bulldozed a road
> down the center of my mind."*
> ~ **Maya Angelou**

Although I have made my peace with my own journey, that question still haunts me as I see us, as a nation, pushing the same knowledge I was denied as a child back into the dark chambers of the underground. My own son hated Black History Month class discussions because, as one of four Black students in his class, he was automatically thought to be the expert in All Things Black—at nine years old. He hated having all eyes on him when the teacher asked questions, as if he was the only one that had an answer, as if black history isn't American history that every American should be well versed in. He hated feeling like White kids came from money and power and black people were all slaves. I remember hating it, too. After watching some once-a-year documentary on slavery–the only highlighted Black History theme–some kid would inevitably shame me with "y'all were all slaves" bullying. That kind of drip-drip-drip painful noise makes wounds that we carry with us. They mostly heal over, but only mostly. And when books are banned and discussions on "sensitive" topics are censored, those wounds tend to ache.

How do I use my journey to show others the damage we do to others when their stories are hidden away? How do I use my voice in rooms where everyone there just wants me to be silent?

I don't have any answers. But I know that there's more knowledge out there than there is clean air.

I have learned that. Yes, my formal education was severely lacking. I was given a bright and shiny version of my country's history, a version that put some on a pedestal, cast some unfairly as enemies, and left some out altogether. I've learned that the desire to maintain that version of America as the only one we present in classrooms is strong and comes from powerful and wealthy people. But I also know that I no longer need a public library to find the truth. And it seems that many young people no longer trust what's in textbooks, so they are leading the charge in research and information dissemination. Taking a page from their playbook, my journey has led me to the research community. Subscriptions to EBSCO and JSTOR are more important than Hulu and Disney, and teachers can access much of the information for free. Additionally, the National Park Service and the Smithsonian are both free, and they provide incredible collections of videos, audio, images, artifacts, and many primary resources so that I can learn about diverse American stories from an insider's perspective.

I'll never know why I have been a recurring One Black Friend. From the little girl in grade school to the teacher in a school building in a little Swiss village to the teacher and music director at a small Lutheran church during the 2016 election, I have learned many lessons.

The most important one is, when something keeps happening, what can you learn from it?

Looking back on my childhood, I have learned that you probably must go along to get along. I hate knowing that. I intensely dislike the fact that, in many instances, Jaquanna won't get an interview, but Jackie will. It's sad to know that gay teachers in certain states can't put family pictures on their desks. It's sad to see many teachers of emerging bilinguals still referring to Language 1 like it's a hindrance and not a benefit. However, I have also learned that by gaining enough power, wealth, or status, you can bypass those gatekeepers. Activist and House Representative AOC wears hoop earrings and red lipstick, which empowered me to do the same in business settings. SCOTUS Judge Ketanji Jackson wears naturally styled locks, as do I. This was a big win over the day I was pulled into my boss's office and asked how long my hair, then braided, would be "like that." I've learned to say, "Your experience may be different than mine," as a period, not a comma, without rancor, and be okay with it. Mostly, I have learned that folks who want to learn will, and those who don't will do everything they can to maintain the status quo. I've learned to be okay with that, too.

I don't come from a family who went to marches and sit-ins. My mother spoke up, but she moved within her "racial" circle, so she was protected in that sense. My grandmother taught me to be quiet and not make waves. She would have kept me in that same circle where I was safe and protected. But there was too much of my mother in me. She was not one to mince words or sugar-coat the truth. While the voice of my grandmother saying, "Always be a lady," is annoyingly stuck in my head at times, it is for her and the women whom she comforted after their sons were lost to racial violence that I speak.

Like the women of that generation, I understand that going along to get along will always be a part of navigating the social constructs that make some folks 'US' and some folks 'THEM'. But like my mother, I have a voice, and silence isn't an option. So, as a recurring One Black Friend, I have learned to find that voice and use it. Why do I keep ending up in spaces in which I am the only one who looks like me? Because I have enough of my grandmother's 'go along' in me to be accepted into those circles. That's something that makes me overthink many of my interactions with others:

Am I going along because it's easier because I am afraid to lose my seat at the table?

Or am I here because my voice is needed in this room, and this is the only way in?

Am I giving up too much of myself?

Am I still being true to myself?

Will those who look like me see me as inauthentic?

Will I like who I see in the mirror tomorrow?

Should I just say no because this exchange is too costly on a personal level?

Being the One Black Friend in these times falls between complicated and downright perilous. I have been in spaces that, after 2016, no longer felt safe. I have also been in spaces where I knew exactly why I was there and what my calling was. Mostly, however, being the OBF falls somewhere in between. S

Sometimes, I feel every bit like a child at that red light, looking at the flag and realizing that the room I have been in is not designed to support me. Sometimes, I just peep in and know immediately. There is nothing to see here, folks. But in this journey, the best moments are when I find myself in a room where, like my mom at that red light, I get to kindly say, "Hello, do you know what that is?" and I get to watch scales drop from eyes and lightbulbs go on overheads all over the room.

Wonderings

Although experiences help shape us, and although I am grateful for my journey, I wonder if we can do better for this generation and the ones to come by ensuring that we tell the whole truth about who we are as a country.

I wonder if we can free up young minds for creativity and achievement by allowing them to be who they are without labelling, judging, or comparing them to an "American Standard" that has been designed by those in power to act as a gatekeeping mechanism?

How can we ensure that students who may not see themselves reflected in curriculum and media don't feel they have to go along to get along?

HEDREICH NICHOLS

Hedreich Nichols is an author, educator, and consultant helping educators and districts amplify the voices of all students.

Hedreich's YouTube series and podcast, SmallBites, further help campuses amplify student voices by focusing on equity in education. Between SmallBites and her work as a writer, Hedreich works to help educators create more culturally responsive classrooms and campuses. Her Cherry Lake trade titles "What is Antiracism?", "What is the Black Lives Matter Movement?" and more provide teachers with materials to help students understand systemic inequities, and her upcoming Solution Tree title, Finding Your Blind Spots, provides educators with guiding principles to help them create more inclusive, welcoming campuses for all students.

As a speaker and keynoter, Hedreich provides educators with inspiration and a safe space to move beyond conversations around race, giving them hands-on, research-based strategies that can be immediately implemented. You can learn more about Hedreich at https://hedreich.com/

Twitter (X): @hedreich

Instagram: @hedreichnichols

Facebook: Hedreich Nichols

LinkedIn: Hedreich Nichols

Rethinking Learning Episode #127:
Amplify the Voices All Students bit.ly/episode127-nichols

Reflection #16: Where are you on your journey to understanding racism? bit.ly/journey2antiracism

11

Spreading Magic
Wherever We Go

ERIKA SANDSTROM 🌱

*"You can't stop the waves, but
you CAN learn to surf!"*
~ Jon Kabat-Zinn

As I reminisce about my journey, I can't help but chuckle at the colorful twists and turns that led me to become a creative educator. You see, creativity and the thirst for trying new things were etched into my being from a young age. My family was a tapestry of artists and crafters, with both my parents and three sisters weaving their magic with artistic finesse. One of my sisters even took her passion to the professional level, becoming a skilled photographer with an MFA from Pratt in illustration. Growing up surrounded by such talented souls, the fear of trying new artistic endeavors was a foreign concept for us. We were a bunch of little creatives ready to take on the world without hesitation.

My childhood was a whirlwind of artistic adventures, like when I took charge of my sister's birthday parties, transforming the front yard into a wonderland of fun and excitement. While Mom was busy planning another celebration in the backyard, I was donning my bright Kelly-green shirt, a not-so-coincidental nod to my future identity as Green Screen Gal, the educator in the making.

Fast forward a few years, and life took me on some unexpected detours. For two decades, I found myself as a yoga and Pilates instructor, with a side gig as a bartender, because life needs that perfect blend of balance and mixology. Little did I know that my world would be turned upside down, leading me to the breathtaking realm of deep breathing and yoga.

A personal injury and some emotional challenges opened my eyes to the transformative power of the mind. I discovered that sitting on a yoga mat and focusing on your breath could be more magical than any potion in a wizard's cauldron. With the wisdom of firsthand experience, I shared my love for yoga far and wide, hoping to sprinkle some magic wherever I went and helping anxious kids find their inner calm one yoga pose at a time.

When I was travelling, my inner artist certainly started to come out again through photography and creative videography. I even took some painting classes and started using oils to paint something for each member of my family, capturing their homes or their views! I was obsessed with painting; however, like always, the inner teacher/leader came out in me again. I was visiting my friend Kimberly in Colorado one summer, and she suggested we go to this place where you paint on a canvas and drink wine. What a concept this "paint and sip" was, and it had certainly not hit the East Coast yet!

Of course, being the ADHD woman, I am with a zillion ideas; I decided that Boston needed one of these places for people to unleash their inner creativity and fall in love with painting like I did. I know I am an entrepreneur at heart, as this has not been the only creative business venture I have embarked upon. When I created the first travelling paint party business in the Boston area, I had NO clue how big it would get and how fast. I was hosting parties in restaurants and churches and even on big stages 3-4 nights a week. YUP, I was one TIRED teacher for sure, but I was so inspired by what all of these experiences taught me.

Truth be told, I was in love with being on stage, inspiring others to tap into their innate creativity, but also because my jokes were fresh every evening. The extroverted LEO IN ME LOVES THE SPOTLIGHT! The pub became a platform for me to unleash the power of the mind and unlock the creative genius within people. We even organized a bash for ALS with three hundred enthusiastic partygoers, all celebrating creativity and supporting a great cause. This made me realize I wanted to be a speaker who helps others use their unique creativity to HEAL.

102

Before, during, and after all these creative adventures, I spent twenty years as a yoga and Pilates instructor and working as a bartender on the side because life needs balance.

While on my yogini journey, I stumbled upon the incredible benefits of deep breathing and yoga. It all started when I faced a personal injury and some emotional challenges. Yet, guess what? Yoga and the power of breath came to my rescue, showing me the transformative power of the mind.

Who could have imagined that simply sitting on a mat and focusing on your breath could be so impactful?

I certainly didn't until I experienced it firsthand. I continued over the years to share my yoga love everywhere and with anyone I could, that would let me.

As a Yoga instructor, I was great at practicing the peace and present moment while I was on the mat teaching and practicing. As soon as I left it, it seemed my world went right back to an autopilot "fight or flight" mode. I wasn't quite aware of the constant opportunities for the healing power of mindfulness since I was a pro at turning it on as soon as I stepped on the mat. However, it seemed to shut off just as quickly when I stepped back into my autopilot ways. Now, after a life-changing and kismet encounter, I know that "you can't stop the waves, but you can learn to surf!" I found the surfboard can be used as a metaphor for my daily Mindfulness practice.

Mindfulness? The buzzword everywhere had a lot deeper meaning and heart than I gave it credit for. It all started with a "chance" (that I know was kismet) meeting in the Toronto airport as the universe CLEARLY had another plan for me.

One fateful day, amidst delays and chaos, I crossed paths with the ever-positive Dr. Blaise Aguierre. With his intriguing South African accent and boundless excitement for life, he radiated mindfulness like a sunbeam on a cloudy day. He taught me the art of riding life's waves— "you can't stop the waves, but you can learn to surf!" And boy, did we surf through that crazy airport adventure, turning my overpacking mishap into a stroke of good fortune. Little did I know that I was entering a new frontier in my life.

Speaking of frontiers, let's talk about my packing skills or lack thereof. I must have been the unofficial President of Over Packers Anonymous. Every time I travelled, my suitcase exploded into a yard sale on the airport floor. The universe seemed to delight in challenging my organizational abilities, but little did I know that my packing fiasco would lead to a miraculous solution and a friendship that would change my life forever.

Enter Dr. Blaise Aguierre, the ever-positive and adventure-loving soul who embraced life with the enthusiasm of a kid in a candy store. Despite the airport chaos and flight delays, he remained as calm as a Zen master on a mountaintop. Meanwhile, there I was, in full victim mode, ready to write a novel about my travel misadventures. Then Blaise, with his inspiring positivity, reminded me that life is an adventure, and every twist and turn is an opportunity to surf the waves of mindfulness.

So, there I stood, meditating with Oprah and Deepak on my phone while my bag transformed into a yard sale display on the airport floor. I must have looked like a tech-savvy yoga guru trying to find my zen amidst the chaos. If mindfulness can survive the chaos of an airport, it can survive anything,

The universe seemed to wink at me when I made a spur-of-the-moment comment about Blaise resembling the Dog Whisperer. I mean, who even says that? Little did I know that it would lead to the revelation that my new friend had appeared in a documentary with none other than Cesar Milan himself. Talk about a small world, or perhaps a world that's interconnected in magical ways we can't always see.

Through it all, the laughter, the mishaps, and the unexpected encounters, I learned that life is too short to take it too seriously. Laughter truly is the best medicine, and in the whirlwind of green screens and mindfulness, I found a perfect recipe for spreading joy and inspiration to others.

Blaise's mentorship and friendship forever changed me, igniting a true mindfulness practice that became my guiding light. Gratitude journals and the power of living in the present moment became my mantra. As I embarked on my journey as a true mindful educator, my heart overflowed with a desire to share this transformative magic with others.

With a sprinkle of humor, a touch of zany ideas, and a heart full of inspiration, I embrace the whimsical world of green screen magic. At an assisted living facility, I brought my magical green screen to capture cool photos, but little did I know it would unleash a wave of joy and playfulness. Elderly individuals with walkers and wheelchairs became daring bungee jumpers, fearless skiers, and intrepid adventurers, all thanks to the power of green screen technology. The BEST part of it all is that the wheelchairs, walkers, and canes disappeared, providing an opportunity for photos and videos these beautiful souls never thought they would see themselves in on this journey of life.

Age melted away, revealing the child within us all, yearning to break free and embrace life's journey.

Who knew a simple screen could bring out the adrenaline junkie in the elderly? All jokes aside, amidst the laughter and playful antics, something magical was happening. We were rediscovering the joy of play, no matter our age or physical limitations. In a world that often takes itself too seriously, the green screen became a portal to the whimsical realm of imagination.

Let me tell you, there's no better feeling than seeing the twinkle in as they unleash their inner child and explore new frontiers.

As I continue my journey as Green Screen Gal, the mindful educator, I hope to infuse every moment with humor, charm, and the heart-warming power of laughter. Life's too short to be a serious grown-up all the time. Let's embrace the child within us, surf the waves of mindfulness, and spread magic wherever we go.

Because in the end, it's not about the awards or recognition, but the joy of knowing that we've touched lives and made the world a little brighter, one laugh and #MyBreathingBubble at a time. Click on the link below to use the Breathing Bubble.

Video of Breathing Bubble
https://youtu.be/pJYu2brzPJc

Let's make this journey unforgettable,
my fellow adventurers!

ERIKA SANDSTROM

Erika Sandstrom is in her 32nd year as an educator in grades 3-8 in several subject areas. Her experience includes eight years of teaching in Missouri, and her 21st year in the Peabody Public Schools teaching grades 6th-8th as a Digital Media Teacher and was the Yearbook Manager for three years.

Erika also serves on the district Technology Team and is a Mindfulness Coach for Peabody, where she launched the Mindful Superhero Club district wide. She is also a Delegation Leader for People to People International and travelled to sixteen countries with students.

Erika is a Digital Learning Coach and Digital Media Teacher specializing in Green Screen and Video Production. Dubbed "Green Screen Gal," Erika shares her creative media and mindfulness passions as a featured speaker at conferences, provides district professional development, hosts online webinars, and created and co-hosted the annual Green Screen Summits.

Erika is a Green Screen and Video Production PD instructor for MASSCUE and https://www.pdcollab.org/, which provides PD and services to 160 school districts in Massachusetts. She works with WeVideo to create SEL lessons for their classroom feature and is a Canvassador for Canva as one of 19 in the US. She recently was featured on the cover of the EdTech K12 Magazine.

LinkTree: https://linktr.ee/greenscreengal44
Twitter (X): @GreenScreenGal
Instagram: @GreenScreenGal44
Facebook: Facebook.com/greenscreengal
LinkedIn: www.linkedin.com/in/erikleeasandstrom
YouTube: https://www.youtube.com/c/erikasandstrom
Website: GreenScreenGal.com
Bio: www.greenscreengal.com/green-screen

Rethinking Learning Podcast #140:
Cultivating Compassion through Creativity
bit.ly/episode140-sandstrom

12

An Unlikely Journey: From Reluctant Teacher to School Leader

CHARLES WILLIAMS

"Your life is your story, and the adventure
ahead of you is the journey to fulfill
your own purpose and potential."
~ Denzel Washington

W hat were you told you should be when you grew up? A
doctor? A lawyer? Whatever you wanted to be? For as
long as I can remember, my grandmother insisted that I would
become an educator. Instead of embracing this dream for my
own and leaning into the journey, I pushed back with everything
I could muster.

A teacher? Me? No way! I could barely stand kids, and I had
no desire to remain in school any longer than necessary,
regardless of how well I did.

My dream was to become a marine biologist. Or maybe an
architect. Or even a public relations specialist. And yet, I am
wrapping up my seventeenth year in education.

How did I get here?

Growing up, I excelled in school. I was always on the honor roll, and because I found the academic load to be fairly easy, I challenged myself by engaging in numerous extracurricular activities, including both athletics and scholarly organizations. I pursued quarterbacks as a linebacker and memorized lines for school plays. I grappled with opponents on the wrestling mat and wrestled with questions during decathlons. I ran relays during track and tracked data for the Science Olympiad.

It was this combination of skills that aligned me with my very first job as a teacher's assistant for a summer school program during the break between middle school and high school. I spent weeks working with students and challenging them to grow academically while also pushing their creative and athletic abilities. The best part was working alongside one of my favorite teachers, who I never had the opportunity to have in school. It was a great experience, but, in my mind, it was nothing more than my first job.

Over the next several years, I held several jobs in several different fields, including selling windows and siding to homeowners while they attempted to shop at KMart, selling overpriced vacuums to customers who just wanted a free demonstration so that they could get a room professionally cleaned, and selling bougie products that promised to deliver all sorts of results to the upscale shoppers at Nordstrom Spa. I did a lot of selling.

I say all of this because I need you to know two things about me at this point in my life. I was a scholar who excelled at school, and I was a worker because my family struggled financially.

During my senior year in high school, I was offered a full scholarship to Ball State University in Muncie, IN, along with being accepted into the honors program and their highly competitive theater program. It was February. It was a dream come true for a first-generation college student. It was also a dream that was about to get a healthy dose of reality. When I came home and shared this news with my then-girlfriend, she dropped two words that would forever alter my journey.

"I'm pregnant."

She insisted that I pursue this wonderful opportunity and assured me that she would be okay, repeatedly saying, *"You don't have to do this."*

But I did have to do this. You see, my father was not present during my childhood, and I could not do the same thing to my own child. As much as I would love to say that this revelation was immediate, I struggled with making a decision as I explored various pathways that would allow me to take advantage of the presented offers while simultaneously playing an active role in my child's life. Ultimately, I opted to remain at home and attend school at the local branch of Purdue University.

Fast forward four years, and I am a senior in college with two daughters and no partner. In fact, I was a single father, sharing custody with my ex-wife while attending school fulltime and working full-time. As my final year came to an end, I attended one of the many job fairs and was presented with two offers.

One position was for a public relations specialist at the casino. The job was newly created to explore the need for the role and was thus presented as a six-month contract with the potential for an extension. This would mean that the job could end on December 1st. Two kids? No job? Looming Christmas?

The second position was for a public relations specialist in the school district that I attended. It would pay a few dollars less per hour, but the position was guaranteed. I accepted.

Initially, I was putting that college degree to work and providing PR support to the Bilingual Education Program as we focused on improving the negative perceptions of a program that catered to immigrant families. In time, however, I was asked if I could provide some support within the classroom and implement the skills garnered from my secondary major in English; I was more than happy to assist.

And that is when it happened. The very prediction that my grandmother had made eight years earlier came true. I was serving as an educator.

This was just the beginning of my journey.

Being back in the classroom provided me with an opportunity to not only see education from the perspective of a teacher but also allowed me to reflect on my time in school. It was at this point that I came to a sobering and humbling realization.

I was not successful in school because I was better than anyone else. I was successful because I fit the mold.

As we know, traditional approaches to education rely heavily on compliance, conformity, and comprehension. Students are expected to know and follow both explicit and unspoken rules and norms. They are praised and rewarded for adhering to codes of conduct and displaying admirable character traits. They are encouraged to process information through reading texts and listening to lectures. I was this student.

It was during this epiphany that I simultaneously realized that some of my peers and even my own brother did not struggle in school because they were not academically gifted but because they were not afforded the same opportunities as I was - to engage in a manner that was consistent with my preferred learning style.

This newfound understanding served as the catalyst for my own approach to teaching students in my classroom. I never wanted any of my students to feel as though they were incapable of learning or achieving academic success. Because of this, I built entire units and a whole curriculum from scratch every year so that I could ensure that the materials we were using not only matched my students' interests but also aligned with their various learning styles.

My efforts paid off. My students, despite being immigrant students who faced the duality of not only learning academic content but also the acquisition of a new language, consistently met their Adequate Yearly Progress (AYP) Goals.

In time, I transitioned into other educational spaces, including a mainstream ELA class, an Honors ELA class, and a Credit Recovery ELA class. In each of these classes, I used similar strategies and ensured that the curriculum we used was uniquely catered to the students in the classroom. In each of these spaces, my students experienced success, often surpassing their peers across the district on statewide assessments.

After spending approximately five years in the classroom, I started to become frustrated with the educational system on a larger scale. The efforts that I was implementing in my classrooms, while not easy, consistently resulted in students making impressive progress. Why, then, were these same students struggling in other classrooms within my building? Why were other teachers so reluctant to shift their practices if it would result in better outcomes? What could I do about this?

I decided to return to school to pursue my second Master's: this one in Educational Administration. It was also at this time that I set an ambitious goal for myself. I wanted to be an administrator by the time I was 30.

You know that adage, "Be careful what you wish for"? Yeah…

During the final months of my seventh year of teaching, I was asked to serve as the interim Assistant Principal for the Middle School wing of our 7-12 building. I accepted and was asked to assume the role officially that summer.

I had done it! I was a school administrator and did so several months before my 30th birthday.

The following summer, while visiting schools in China through a partnership with the Confucius Institute out of Valparaiso University, I received word that my principal was resigning.

Stepping down? How could this be? We had a plan. I would grow under her guidance. She would shape me into a leader so that I would, one day, be prepared to assume her role. We spent less than one year together.

I was confused. I was scared. I was frustrated. I called her. She explained why she was stepping down and encouraged me to take the position. Me? Who was I to be the principal of a high school?

No way. Nope. Not me.

The interview process was daunting, and I was surprised when I received a call to see the CEO of our management company. He explained that he wanted me to take the position and shared that he saw in me much of what he saw in himself at my age. A young leader full of potential and the gumption to challenge norms in order to move the company forward.

And well... here I am ten years later, writing this chapter.

I shared this story because I want you to take away two key lessons:

1. *Opportunity meets Preparation:*

Rarely will you ever feel truly ready for the opportunities that present themselves to you. But know that success happens when opportunity meets preparation. You must consistently develop yourself into the person you want to become. You must take advantage of as many opportunities to learn and grow into and beyond your comfort zone. I didn't feel ready to accept these challenges - whether it was stepping into the classroom for the first time without any formal training or accepting the role of the head of a school with only one year of administrative experience. And yet, I did the work necessary to equip myself with the knowledge and skills that would support me through the myriad of struggles that I faced along the way. Without that vital preparation, these opportunities would have resulted in failure.

2. Challenge the Status Quo:

In whatever space you find yourself, you will undoubtedly discover the status quo - the collection of processes, ideas, and practices that are ever present within an organization. Oftentimes, nobody knows when they started, how they began, or why they remain. What is collectively understood is that they represent a very common response -"That's the way we've always done it." Let me be clear, I HATE this phrase. The mere existence of a thing does not, and should not, justify its continued presence. Many organizations, however, choose not to engage in the uncomfortable practice of engaging in self-reflection to question whether these status quo items deserve to remain.

If you are going to be a leader, you must be willing to challenge the status quo. Otherwise, you will end up being a manager. You must be willing to ask difficult questions and propose unpopular solutions. It is within this realm of uncomfortableness where true change can happen. This is how I was able to adopt practices that my colleagues ignored. This is how I was able to replicate these same approaches when I became a school leader so that the successes within my classroom were now experienced across the building.

Be brave enough to push back on systems and structures that do not support those that you serve.

CHARLES WILLIAMS

Charles Williams has been an educator for nearly 20 years, serving as a teacher, a mentor/lead teacher, an assistant principal, and a principal for urban students in grades K-12.

He also serves as an equity advocate through his work with Great Expectations Mentoring, Chicago Public School's Office of Equity, and The City of Chicago's Equity Office.

Charles is the host of The Counter Narrative Podcast, a show designed to challenge the dominant narrative that often negatively portrays our disenfranchised population, and the co-host of Inside the Principal's Office, a bi-monthly show featuring educational leaders from around the world. He is also one of the co-authors of "Inside the Principal's Office: A Leadership Guide to Inspire Reflection and Growth."

After presenting at numerous nationwide conferences, educational workshops, and fundraising events, Charles decided to launch CW Consulting - an organization committed to delivering personalized keynotes, workshops, and consulting services focused on helping institutions unlock their potential and deliver results.

Twitter (X): @_cwconsulting

Contact info: linktr.ee/_cwconsulting

LinkedIn: https://www.linkedin.com/in/charlesmwilliamsjr/

Website: http://www.cwconsultingservice.com/

Rethinking Learning Podcast Episode #141:
Intersection of Education, Leadership, and Equity
https://bit.ly/episode141-williams

13

Educating with Hope, Optimism and Courage: A Journey from Cynicism to Possibility

JENNIFER D. KLEIN

"I was raised to know every open wound on this earth is a wound of mine, and every time I'm on my knees refusing to stand and be a healer, I may as well be the disease."
~ **Andrea Gibson**

I don't think I've ever written anything with a happy ending. I remember writing a short story in 3rd grade about a frog who tried to cross a road—and failed. My teacher seemed concerned.

"Why didn't you let the frog get to the other side?" he asked.

"It's obvious," I insisted. "The road is wide, and the frog is small—it's totally unrealistic to think he'd make it."

My parents got a call that night from my teacher. "Your daughter is a talented young writer... but you should probably know that her worldview is a little dark for an eight-year-old."

Years later, as a student of creative writing with a focus on fiction, I heard something similar from my senior project committee in college and during my graduate school thesis defense: "You're a good writer, but your vision of the world is too dark, and your characters aren't likable enough for the reader to want them to succeed." When I submitted the first draft of my first book on education decades later, my editor told me I needed to emphasize constructive practices more than criticize current ones; much of my work on *The Global Education Guidebook* was a personal journey toward a more optimistic narrative that, though critical, celebrated what was possible.

I grew up in a family of activists. My parents were basically the Jewish intellectual version of hippies, and they raised us to act on our beliefs. We didn't touch Nestle products throughout my childhood because of the baby formula scandal of the early 1970s and their manipulation of poor women in Africa. We avoided green grapes for over a decade in support of migrant workers during the César Chavez boycott movement. My family wouldn't even travel to Arizona because the state never passed the Equal Rights Amendment. All of this had its base in Jewish thought and law: it was not okay to celebrate your own wellbeing if your neighbors were in need, ever. It was as simple as that. But I can't say that the nightly news demonstrated much of this value in action.

For most of my life, I described myself as a "cynical idealist." I wanted to believe that things could turn out better and that humans might make better choices, but I never really expected them to. I learned to blend at school by noticing when my peers thought I was being too dark—and not sharing those kinds of insights anymore. But I still had them, and I wanted to be a writer because it seemed safer to have serious thoughts on paper than to say them out loud. My parents sent me to an alternative school, the Open School in Colorado, and yes, it was a place that accepted differences. But even so, I quickly learned which kinds of differences were most acceptable.

I remember hundreds of breakdowns in the privacy of my bedroom, especially as my engagement with the world deepened and diversified. Studying the Holocaust led to 5-hour sobbing sessions—I can only imagine how hard it was for my parents to figure out how to help. I tried to ensure they were the only ones who saw this part of me, the sensitive heart ripped to shreds by the smallest unkind act, a heart that nearly burst when my little sister lost her favorite toy or got bullied at school. By the time I left for the Middle East at the end of my junior year of high school, I had perfected the blithe smile my peers and teachers expected, but disappointment and sadness were always simmering beneath the surface.

I lived in Israel/Palestine for six months in 1985, followed by two months backpacking around Europe and Britain. I completed three independent projects for high school in those eight months. But honestly, I barely remember any of that. What I remember is drinking tea among Israeli and Palestinian youth in East Jerusalem and what a relief it was in comparison to the tensions, slurs, and division I saw on the streets most days—all of which contradicted what I'd been raised to believe about our collective responsibility to ensure our neighbors' well-being as much as our own.

I have a particularly clear memory of coming upon a gathering of Ethiopian Jews in West Jerusalem one evening, recent refugees who were protesting for their rights. My Global Awareness passage had been focused on their evacuation from Ethiopia and the legal and social hurdles they were facing in

Israel. I watched for hours from the periphery; in my memory, they were all dressed in white, playing music and dancing and singing. At 17, it was easily the most beautiful thing I'd ever witnessed, so beautiful it made me weep. And I remember thinking that none of it made sense—the division and anger among so many ethnic groups who just wanted a piece of hallowed land and a bit of God to call their own—especially when such beauty was possible.

Something broke in me during those months, something I couldn't put into words. I lost my faith in God along with my faith in humans; I didn't want to follow a God who allowed her name to be the excuse for violence and hatred (and yes, my feminist parents always referred to God as female). I'm not sure exactly when it happened when that psychic crack grew out of my control. What I saw in those months broke my heart and made me turn inward more than ever. I also fell in love for the first time during that trip with a young woman from Luxemburg who suddenly became a born-again Christian in the middle of our love affair and told me I'd go to hell. And so I had my heart broken for the first time during those months as well.

I came home shortly before my 18th birthday, struggling to live with my ability to step away from hatred and conflict when the people I'd come to love in the region didn't and couldn't. I wanted to understand how to turn hate and bigotry into something powerful and constructive, but I didn't know how. Heartbroken, with my **faith** in basically everything shattered, all I knew was that humans had more capacity for hatred than for love and that we built barriers more than bridges. And if this was our true nature, I wanted nothing more to do with any of it.

Reentry into the United States was much harder than living in a conflict region. I cried myself to sleep every night, confused by how a God I was raised to see as kind could be an excuse for hatred and violence. I considered suicide repeatedly because I didn't know how to live in a world populated by so much horror. My friends asked why I'd become so serious suddenly when, in truth, I'd been serious **my** whole life—I'd just learned to hide it. At 18, I was finished hiding anything. My teachers did their best to help me process my experience, but I didn't know how to tell the story or even what story to tell. My parents, whose parents were members of the Boston Zionist Movement, didn't know what to do with me, particularly once I declared I was an atheist and would no longer self-identify as Jewish. I stopped going to classes consistently and started retreating into books more and more. I got stoned in the woods near my high school every day, had casual sex to feel alive, and tried to forget more than understand what was wrong with the world and what was missing in my heart.

I spent the next eight years with blinders on. I disconnected from the world, and after an education rich with cultural immersion, I turned away from the world completely. I didn't study abroad during college, immersing myself instead in the world of literature and writing. When ugly human nature reared its head in a book, I could close the cover and walk away. When I wrote the story myself, I got to decide how it ended—and I became the queen of unhappy endings, as I hoped my writing might help others see what I was now so conscious of, that humans only practiced kindness and concern for others selectively, and that we were all, in the words of William Golding, *"suffering from the terrible disease of being human."*

But nearly a decade later, at the age of 26, I walked into my first high school classroom, and everything changed. I'd taught college-level writing to put myself through graduate school, but I'd spent those years assuming I'd become a professional writer. I was surrounded by talent in school and had been fed the dominant narrative that teachers were people who couldn't fulfill their real purpose. But I moved to Costa Rica without a job, and what I now know was a sort of leap off the ledge and back into the world that I never expected to survive. So, I said yes when a prestigious international school offered me a position teaching 10th-grade English and American Literature. I figured I'd spend a year or two teaching and have something worthy of publishing by the time I left. But I never really left. My students changed the stories I wanted to tell; their stories took over the narrative.

Suddenly, I wanted to hear every fascinating, messy idea that might come from their fascinating, messy minds—and I wanted to write about what it looked like to bring out the best in them, as my teachers tried to do for me. It turned out I knew how to ask the right questions, how to listen, and how to believe them when they were honest about themselves.

We put our desks in a circle and moved them back into rows at the end of every class for the math teacher I shared the room with. I went home every day covered in colored dry-erase residue and had to throw away everything white I owned. I tried to bring out the best in them; I tried to make them care about everything, to make them want to change the world. I knew they *would* change the world. I don't remember waking up one morning feeling optimistic about the world, but I do remember a growing sense of possibility. And then I was marking student essays one weekend, and my boyfriend noticed a particular name on one of them.

"Did I know who that was?" he asked. I shook my head.

"His father won the Nobel Peace Prize," he told me. "You're teaching the son of a president."

The following week at school, I paid more attention to my class lists. It wasn't just one student who was the child of a president; there were several. I also had the nephew of the Minister of Education in my classroom, the children of major thought leaders and business owners. And it no longer mattered whether I could personally change or even live with the world as it was; I now understood the last part of my high school's goals: I had a chance *to create the world that ought to be.* If my students remembered anything I taught them and carried anything away from their experiences with me, then the dark side of humanity would never win; *they* would.

An old friend of my mom's recently assumed that the shift away from fiction writing was a sad one, a departure from my true purpose. But that is far from true. I found my purpose when I became an educator; those young people turned me into someone who believes something better is possible and who writes and facilitates learning every day to help make it happen. I still don't believe in happy endings. But 23 years after my heart was broken by the human condition, I returned to the Middle East to teach poetry in the West Bank. And I realized, thanks to a Palestinian friend who helped me reframe my worldview, that I am actually a broken-hearted optimist. I want so much to believe that humans are capable of goodness that every act of violence and hatred rocks me to the core.

Injustice still leaves me in a blubbering pile on the floor of my bathroom, just as I fell to pieces the first time a kid in the neighborhood tried to beat up my little sister. But I work every day toward something better, and I believe that better is possible.

I embrace what school **leaders** shared during the research for my second book, *The Landscape Model of Learning*, that education requires an unending supply of hope, optimism, and courage. The work of educators is exhausting and frustrating. It requires more hope, optimism, and courage than I have most days. But I can't think of anything I would rather do.

Humans are capable of extraordinary kindness and beauty, and education can help foster **that** by creating schools where every child thrives and societies where every human finds purpose and joy, free from the threat of hatred and conflict.

This will be my legacy. This will be my happy ending.

JENNIFER D. KLEIN

Jennifer D. Klein is a product of experiential project-based education herself, and she lives and breathes the student-centered pedagogies used to educate her. She became a teacher during graduate school in 1990, quickly finding the intersection between her love of writing and her fascination with educational transformation and its potential impact on social change.

Jennifer is a former head of school with extensive international experience and over 30 years in education—including 19 years in the classroom—with five years in Costa Rica and three in Colombia. She facilitates dynamic, interactive workshops for teachers, leaders, and students, working to amplify student voice, provide the tools for high-quality project-based learning in all cultural and socio-economic contexts, and shift school culture to support such practices.

Jennifer is also committed to intersecting global project-based learning with culturally responsive and anti-racist teaching practices, and her experience includes deep work with schools seeking to address equity, build a healthier community, and improve identity politics on campus. Jennifer's first book, *The Global Education Guidebook,* was published in 2017, and her second, *The Landscape Model of Learning: Designing Student-Centered Experiences for Cognitive and Cultural Inclusion,* written with co-author Kapono Ciotti, was published in 2022.

As an educational leader, writer, speaker, and bilingual workshop facilitator, Jennifer strives to inspire educators to shift their practices in schools worldwide.

To learn more about Jennifer's work and books, visit
PRINCIPLED Learning Strategies at
https://principledlearning.org
and follow her at @jdeborahklein on
Twitter (X), Instagram, and LinkedIn.

Rethinking Learning Podcast: Episode #151:
Educating with Hope, Optimism and Courage
https://bit.ly/episode151-klein

14

Getting Past Gatekeepers by Finding and Living Your Why

When people show you who they are, believe them.
~ **Maya Angelou**

Gatekeepers exist in every profession and stage of life. They are the ones letting you in or out of a place you want to go. There are a lot of different kinds of gatekeepers in the world, and some educators are drawn to the gatekeeper style of leadership. This can play out in the classroom, the school, or even at the board/district level. Gatekeepers use their positional power to help create opportunities or put-up barriers. We all encounter gatekeepers of varying degrees in education, and knowing our *whys* can help us manage them and keep ourselves going to get past them.

Defining your *why* is an important contributor to living a meaningful and purposeful life. You may spend a lot of time figuring out who you are and gaining clarity on what motivates you, as well as where you want to go. On that journey, there are people who may stand in your way. Some might be doing it to help you deepen your conviction and become even clearer on your *why*, while others may be motivated by their mere ability to control access. Others, still, may have malicious intent. I have realized after years of good mistakes, and a lot of practice overcoming challenges that getting past a gatekeeper requires asking their *why*.

It's not easy to tell a gatekeeper's purpose or their reasoning for holding you back. It took me many years to see that one of my former principals was intentionally keeping me out of formal leadership roles and, eventually, out of options. Finally, realizing why she was doing that helped to mitigate some of the difficulty. It took a lot of heartache, and I was pushed to my absolute limits. Now that I am on the other side, embodying the agency for which I fought so strongly, I hope that my experiences can help others. Leaving my former independent school was among the most difficult and important decisions of my life. I loved my students and their families, I loved the community, and I loved my work. It had all the right ingredients for a wholehearted teaching life, except my principal was standing in the way.

At first, I watched who got through her gate and wondered why *them* and not *me*. Why was a certain person receiving a smile and nod, or why was another person's behavior excused for doing the inexcusable? I pontificated what qualified the golden ticket holders for an open door and safe passage while I kept hitting the wall. I pondered what I needed to do to break through.

Looking back, I should have seen that she disliked me, but I honestly didn't. When I finally realized it, I was so thrown by it that my response was to "kill her with kindness". I tried to be the best I could be at my job, working harder and longer hours than ever before. As an already recognized teacher of excellence, this was way off balance. I tried desperately to please her and convince her of my worth. That tenacity can work with some gatekeepers who get worn down and let you in as a reward for your endurance. They eventually accept you, finally seeing your merit. That *did not* happen in my situation. The harder I tried; the worse things got.

This woman did not like me. It would not be hyperbolic if I used *hate* as the verb to describe it. She told me she didn't like the sound of my voice, she embarrassed me at staff meetings, and she refused to share a compliment with me, even if it was an accolade that I found out about through someone in administration because they felt I deserved to hear it. The list goes on. People tried to help bring me solace by giving me all sorts of reasons why she didn't like me: jealousy, ineptitude, she was just *like* that. It was tearing me apart inside. When an article came out in Canadian Teacher Magazine about my unique teaching approach called Building Outside the Blocks, her answer to reading the piece was, "I read it." I had to reread her email a few times to fathom it as a plausible response. I am deeply impacted by people who don't like me, especially those in authority positions, but how she showed me she didn't like me was something I tried to navigate consciously. I regularly deliberated how to manage this during meetings with my mentor, who would advise me by echoing the words of Maya Angelou: *When people show you who they are, believe them.* I finally saw her clearly and tried to carry on despite the disdain.

Knowing that she was being cruel to me because she didn't like me and that there was nothing I could seem to do to change that was difficult to process, but it helped me.

When gatekeepers show you who they are, you need to use that information to deepen your sense of self, clarify your why, and plan the next steps.

If you want to go somewhere and someone is in your way, you can benefit from knowing *why*, but you can also use that as an opportunity to dive deeper into your own *why*. That seeming stumbling block should initiate a point of reflection to ensure that where you want to go is right for you. Ask yourself:

- Why do you want to go there?
- What will happen if you get there?
- What will happen if you don't?

At that stage of my career, after building a reputation for exemplary teaching for decades, I had a lot to lose. I had tenure and seniority. I was known and respected in my community. As a result, I spent that final year in my school in a cycle that was leaving me more insecure and unsure about my future. My principal started attacking me through job placement:

The not so secret but hard to prove weapon of administrators, and she took away my position of responsibility. I took the principal's course to become an administrator, thinking that would be my ticket out of my situation. I looked for guidance and mediation. I even worked up the guts to tell her to stop. Then, it escalated even more. Somehow, facing her emboldened her loathing. She prevented me from professional opportunities at work, and then she tried to stop me from leaving to pursue the next steps. In a feedback interview with an administrator at a public school board, she told me that I *had* to

133

leave my school. Imagine interviewing for the vice principal pool and being required to use your current principal as a reference when *she* is the reason you need to leave. Then, imagine finding out that your required reference made you sound thoroughly incompetent. I was so jarred by hearing this from a stranger, though she wouldn't tell me exactly what my principal had said about me. Whatever it was bad enough for her to adamantly exclaim that *I needed to leave my school.* That woman shocked me and saved me. I've wanted to thank her so many times for helping me see the truth that I already knew but did not want to admit to myself. I finally came to terms with the fact that leaving was an existential reality.

Although it felt like it would break me at the time, I needed to get beyond my principal's gaze and gate.

It's one thing to know your purpose; it's another thing to live it.

In retrospect, it all seems so clear, but at the time, I was so busy trying to get over this seemingly insurmountable challenge that I couldn't see how it was helping me. Sometimes, you are trying so hard to get through the doorway that you don't stop to ask yourself *why* you wanted to go through there in the first place. I didn't know what I wanted to do next. I saw being a vice principal as my way out, but it wasn't really the job I wanted. Deep down, I knew what I really wanted, but I was afraid to admit it. I love the classroom, and I wanted to stay there. I also wanted to have reach and impact beyond the classroom. There was no leadership role that I knew of that could let me do that in the way that I wanted.

One of my greatest skills is that I can find gaps and create innovative ways to address and bridge them. I was afraid to be true to what had been gnawing at me throughout this time because I also needed the security of a job. If I was to follow the path I wanted to carve out, I needed one foot on the ground while I leaped into the unknown. I swallowed my pride in terms of position and focused on my mission. I needed autonomy and security, which can feel like an oxymoron when it comes to work. I also wanted to do more in education beyond the classroom or school, but I didn't want to leave the classroom. I wanted to teach in public school, to see if I was the teacher I was told I was beyond the hallowed halls of the independent schools where I had worked. That meant starting at an entry-level role as a supply/occasional substitute teacher, and I knew it could take years to get a contract position. Because of everything that happened, I said what I wanted out loud, which started to give me the permission I needed to make it happen. I would not be where I am had I not been forced to go in a new direction. How I got here was something I don't wish on anyone, but there's nowhere else I'd rather be.

After twenty-plus years of teaching in the system I was in, I started over. While I became an occasional teacher/substitute teacher/supply teacher, I also started my consulting practice, Building Outside the Blocks. My principal keeping me out of a lot of different things did help me find my own thing. Self-determination was the fuel that kept me going, and my fresh start was a new lease on my professional life.

I have seen a lot of different gatekeepers in my career. I have seen people at the ready, holding you accountable and opening the door once you have met the criteria for entry. I have seen gatekeepers who let you through and then infinitely remind you that they were the ones who got you to where you are. I have seen gatekeepers who are champions coaching you over the hurdles, and I have seen gatekeepers who remind you that they are gatekeepers merely to reinforce their power. I have heard about other difficult gatekeepers who hold people back because they can, but I have heard of only a few as diabolical as the one I left. I am still trying to move past the anger and hurt, but I also feel sorry for her. If one's power stems from deciding who is in and who is out, how will one ever be a real leader? It's not always meritorious or about criteria when you do get through someone's gate. Sometimes, it's about you, and that is a hard reality to bear. When people stand in your way because they don't want to let *you* through, it forces you to take a long, hard look at yourself.

You should never shrink yourself to
fit into spaces you've outgrown.
~ Author Unknown

I never outgrew my school or my classroom work. I outgrew being told that I wasn't good enough by a person who showed me no respect and was not a person deserving of respect. These system-supported gatekeepers are out of your realm of control, no matter how difficult it can be to manage. I often wonder how many of them got through the gates that brought them to where they are.

Dr. Wayne Dyer said, "What other people think of me is none of my business."

I recognize that the only person's opinion that truly matters is my own. In a professional setting, there can be a lot of value in understanding others' perceptions of you, especially when they are in the role of gatekeeper. Other people have a lot of information to help us on our way to living our purpose. They have details that can support our reflection and our learning. How we are seen by others can help us see ourselves and make the seemingly invisible visible. We just must decide whose opinions to value and recognize that we should not give our power away to those who aren't worth hearing.

Gatekeepers can give you the necessary pause for reflection, help you deepen your *why*, and strengthen your resolve. When you read about all the classic fail-forward stories from successful people, they are often met with a challenge related to someone keeping them out of a place they want to go. Their success, sometimes because of this and sometimes despite it, is propelled by the impasses they have faced and overcome. Tenacity, grit, and a growth mindset help, but gatekeepers can really challenge and throw you off track. Only you, though, can give them the power to derail you.

Not everyone has choices like I did. If you can't get past the gatekeeper because of opportunity, economics, or other limitations, sometimes recognizing that you're in that situation is enough to give you some perspective and space to breathe. You don't have to be a victim of circumstance.

Change your stance and take control of what you can. People will come along, throw you off, and keep you out intentionally or unintentionally.

You don't have to follow their lead; you can go your own way.

In the almost seven years since my self-liberation, I have become a part-time contract teacher on a public board, and my consulting work is growing. I have hosted an epic podcast, which is how I first got to know Barbara Bray. She shared her nostalgia, identity, and pick-me-up songs with me on my former show, The Personal Playlist Podcast (P3), and she interviewed me as I was taking that leap into my consulting work and "building wings on the way". The student version of the P3 project was the focus of my TEDx Talk, Play It Forward, which was a bucket list achievement. I now host a live show with a different panel of educators each week. This broadcast on VoicEd Radio called OnEdMentors is a part of the mentorship community I started called The Mentoree. My consulting work allows me to create projects and initiatives for schools, boards, and communities with the lead team at The Mentoree and through my independent consulting work. I am doing a variety of exciting things.

I have had my third children's book published, and I built the content on the Strum *and The Wild Turkeys* website to help educators and parents use the story to help kids find their voice and rock their differences. I even wrote a song connected to the book that was recorded by a Canadian children's duo and can be found on every streaming platform: "Different is Good" by Sonshine and Broccoli. Much of this happened after I left and because I moved myself forward beyond my situation. I am doing everything I have ever dreamt of and living truer to myself.

Great things were never constructed from comfort zones; try building outside the blocks and see where it takes you.

We need to be our own gatekeepers.

I am getting past this gatekeeper by going from asking, "Why not me?" to "Why me?" to asserting, "Me!"

We need to keep out the people who try to bring us down and keep our core values in view. That should always include believing in yourself. You can learn a lot from gatekeepers and even despite them. I have learned that when things become personal, you must get personal with yourself and your sense of purpose. Know your *why*. If you don't know what that is, start there.

NOA DANIEL

Noa Daniel is a teacher, consultant, speaker, and children's book author. Her third book, *Strum and The Wild Turkeys* includes the theme of inclusion, belonging, and the transformational power of music. Strum's song from the book *"Different is Good"* is now recorded on Canadian music duo Sonshine and Broccoli's new album. Noa teaches part-time in the York Region District School Board.

She supports schools and communities in developing projects and initiatives that amplify the voice and propel engagement through Building Outside the Blocks. Under that umbrella, Noa co-founded The Mentoree, a mentorship community for educators. Through The Mentoree, Noa helps to develop mentorship experiences for educators at any and every stage of their careers in different forms. She hosts OnEdMentors live each week on voicEd Radio, which helps to reflect and inform The Mentoree. Noa is a TEDx and keynote speaker. She is also a director on the board of Learning Forward Ontario.

LinkTree: https://linktr.ee/NoaDaniel

Twitter, Instagram @iamNoaDaniel

Email: noa@buildingoutsidetheblocks.com

Strum and the Wild Turkeys:
https://strumandthewildturkeys.com/

Episode #7: Building Wings on the Way
https://barbarabray.net/2017/08/16/building-wings-on-the-waywith-noa-daniel/

Reflection #17: Becoming the Mentor Kids Deserve
https://bit.ly/reflection17-daniel

15

Direction, Connection, and Growth

KECIA MCDONALD

*"How what I never wanted to be
has become the best of who I am."*

Direction

I would never, ever be a teacher.

That's what I would say if someone queried. I vehemently declared that I would never tread the path of a teacher. With unwavering certainty, I asserted that teaching was not my calling. People would ask me what I wanted to be when I grew up or what I wanted to do in life. The answers ranged from ballerina to first woman President of the United States. Then, unprovoked, I would add, "But I will never be a teacher. I could never teach."

Thus far, I have not been a ballerina or a U.S. President. I have been engaged as an ice cream scooper, a personal shopper, a camp counselor, a resident assistant, a custodial services employee, a human rights advocate, a volunteer, a bed and breakfast owner, a plant nursery and florist operator, a cafe chef

142

and owner, a secretary, and a house fixer upper. My last three job titles are part-time teacher, substitute teacher, and full-time certified teacher.

In 2014, I moved to Hawaii after living in southern Africa for 20 years. I arrived with two kids and two duffel bags, and although I was anchored by my family, in all other aspects, it was a shock. Not only was I transferring my physical residence from one side of the world to another, but I was also entering a post-internet and post-9/11 era. When I left the US in 1994, there was no social media, no OJ Simpson trial, no Sandy Hook.

Additionally, I had done all of my adult "firsts" while living in Africa: getting married, having children, and buying a first home. I landed feeling like a middle-aged fledgling who didn't know how to be an "adult" in this unfamiliar world.

After getting my kids registered for school, my next priority was job hunting. A job at a retail store fit my needs, as the shifts were only four hours long, so I could work around my kids' schedule. In Hawai'i, employers are required to provide benefits for employees who work 20 hours or more, so companies often offer shift work up to 19 hours. Many people work two and three jobs in this capacity, as I did for a while. At some point, a coworker noticed me working 16 hours a week at $9 per hour without benefits and said, "Did you know you can become a substitute teacher if you have a bachelor's degree?"

In a remarkable instant, my "never" transformed into my new direction.

Connection

The journey to becoming a teacher didn't happen overnight. It took time and effort to get established as a part-time teacher, then a substitute, then a fully qualified and certified educator.

I'll admit my initial attraction to the profession was driven by practical considerations like benefits and working hours that matched my children's schedules. People scoff when I say I went into this work for the money, but there's an element of truth to that reality.

The current version of the "What do you want to be when you grow up?" conversation happens regularly at professional learning opportunities; you may know it as a common icebreaker activity. Participants are asked to pair off or get in groups to speak to and celebrate that one teacher who inspired them to join the profession. It's a nice warm-up to bring the spirits of teachers' past into the room, to share our core values and earliest determinations to become an educator, and to remind us of our why. I suppose I could make up a story about one of my favorite teachers to meet the task and contribute to the feel-good intention of the activity. However, I took a different approach and spoke my truth: I became a teacher for the stability it offered and to accommodate my children's needs.

But there's another truth that emerged from within me, one that had always been there despite my vocal opposition: I had been growing my skills as a teacher throughout my journey. During high school, I worked as a summer camp counselor, assisting and mentoring younger kids. At university, I was one of the first sophomores to be approved as a resident assistant in the on-campus housing, so as a second-year student, I was charged with looking after 50 first-year students. As a Peace Corps Volunteer, I was travelling to villages, holding workshops on small-scale agricultural techniques and food preservation projects; I was facilitating adult learning. Looking back, I can now connect the dots and see how my life was always intertwined with aspects of teaching, even when I didn't realize it. It feels like a homecoming, a return to where I was always meant to be. Teaching encapsulates all those acts of helping, guiding, supporting, and empowering that I had been doing unconsciously. It's a fulfilling realization to see how these threads connected and led me to this meaningful profession.

Moreover, teaching has connected me to my community.

Working in the schools gave me a front-row seat to the multi-cultural, multi-lingual, and vast socio-economic range of people who feature in my new home in Hawai'i.

After twenty years spent living outside the US, I felt like I was learning everything all over again. My kids were entering US education for the first time, and we had the opportunity to go through the experience together. Seeing the back end of the school system while simultaneously undergoing the parent version helped me to guide my transplant kids and understand the why behind so many things that happen in a classroom and on a school campus. They were struggling to adjust, and being a teacher who had to be responsive to the needs of a vast array of children helped me to know best how to respond to my own in a way that made sense to them and helped them to settle in. Working with students and families gave me perspective and a deeper understanding to address my own children's experiences and issues. This connected me to them while they were going through some of the most important and foundational moments of their childhood and helped me to understand the community in which they were growing up. It strengthened the bond between me and my children during their formative years, enriching our shared experiences and allowing me to be present for them in meaningful ways.

Growth

Although no one asks me what I want to be when I grow up anymore, I understand that staying in education keeps me on a continuous journey of growth. Although I described becoming a teacher as an unexpected homecoming, it is not a finish line one cross and is "done". I can't think of another profession that requires as much change, learning, and adaptability as education does. Teaching calls for a never-ending cycle of self-improvement and transformation.

Being a teacher has not only shaped my professional life but has also made me a better person. The growth demanded by this role is unparalleled. Teaching requires more learning from me than being a student ever did. As a student, I excelled academically, effortlessly achieving good grades, and earning accolades. However, the traditional education system failed to teach me one crucial skill: how to embrace feedback and correction. It is embarrassing to think about it now how confident I felt because I knew how to get the "right" answers in the traditional classroom. For the greater part of my young adulthood, I saw feedback only as a negative process, as it meant.

I had gotten something "wrong"; all those years of standardized grading taught me that a letter grade with no comments meant everything was okay, but a worksheet or paper with marks on it, or (heaven forbid) a teacher conference could only mean bad news. Being asked for an extension or clarification of my thinking also felt like a challenge, an obvious contravention of my correctness. Accepting feedback was foreign to me and left me feeling undervalued and inadequate.

It is only since becoming a teacher that I realize the importance of critical thinking, curiosity, questioning, and the role of feedback in building better understanding and reaching our full potential. Teaching has taught me the value of failure, learning by doing, making mistakes, and having the resilience to fail forward. I now recognize that we don't invest in what we don't value, and that feedback is fuel for growth and demonstrates someone's belief that you are incredibly capable. The in-progress assessment shows that you can go further and achieve more, and that the commenter is partnering in your success. I don't know that I ever would have realized the transformative power of feedback had I not become a teacher.

During my years as a student, I felt validated by scores and awards, and I didn't really stop to think about how others were experiencing school. Teaching a wide range of children with various skills, backgrounds, and abilities has trained me to look for strengths and merit beyond the grade point average or who can raise their hand the quickest. I grew to recognize the inherent potential in each student. In this way, teaching has also led me to a more just, compassionate, and empathetic perspective. This is why I say being a teacher has made me a better person.

Ralph Waldo Emerson said, "What we fear doing most is usually what we most need to do." In hindsight, my earliest protests against the profession were a measure of self-protection: I didn't give myself enough credit for being up to the job. My initial resistance to teaching was fear that I lacked the ability to adequately serve and do the role justice. I am grateful that life had plans for me beyond those I was making for myself. The path I never saw coming became my course correction.

Wonderings

My teaching journey was instigated by necessity yet was underpinned by a lifetime of experiences and continues with the pull of both personal and professional growth. I no longer stay in the job for the salary or for the ability to work around my kids' schedules. The connections that have been fostered and the understanding of self and others that have come because of this journey go far beyond paychecks and timetables; this is truly a manifestation of my past, present, and future self.

The epitome "never say never" story has turned out to be the ultimate expression of my existence and my why.

Has your why taken you somewhere
you never thought you'd go?

Has your why defined your journey, or
has your journey defined your why?

148

KECIA MCDONALD

Kecia McDonald is a mom, traveler, and educator. She grew up in the Bay Area of California and is a proud graduate of the University of California at Santa Barbara. She joined the Peace Corps after graduating from college. This transformative experience led her to spend two decades in various African countries, immersing herself in different societies, languages, and traditions. It was during this time that Kecia developed an unwavering appreciation for the beauty of diversity and an empathetic understanding of global perspectives. She currently lives in Hawai'i, where she is a public school educator. Having moved 26 times, Kecia is no stranger to change and adaptability. Her experiences abroad and her keen interest in diverse cultures have made her an advocate for cultivating empathy, respect, and global citizenship among her students.

Kecia's passion for teaching led her to specialize in Teen Health, equipping young individuals with crucial life skills and promoting their well-being. She currently serves as a Complex Area Resource Teacher for English Learners across 19 schools. She loves the education profession as it inspires her to constantly learn. She was a Hawaii State Teacher Fellow in 2020-2022 and an NEA Global Learning Fellow in 2022 and is regularly seeking opportunities to improve her professional practice.

Kecia firmly believes that education is a dynamic process that constantly challenges and inspires both students and educators alike. She plans to join the Peace Corps again when she retires from the Hawaii Department of Education. Outside the realm of education, Kecia is an eager traveler and a busy mother. Her experiences as a parent have further strengthened her belief in the transformative power of education and the importance of equipping children with the tools, they need to thrive in an everchanging world.

Twitter (X): @mcdonald_kecia

Reflection #4 Mental Health Awareness All Year Long
https://bit.ly/reflection-keciaandbarbara

Episode #131: Schools Places of Wellness
https://bit.ly/episode131-mcdonald

Section 3

Grow Your Why

What story empowered you to go out of your comfort zone to grow your why?

Each story from the contributing authors in this section is about how they were challenged to push themselves out of their comfort zone. They share how they had to redefine what they were passionate about, what they needed to do to nurture their purpose, and how they advocated for their why.

*"If we're growing, we're always going
to be out of our comfort zone."*
~ John C. Maxwell

16

Eat the Cake!

Dr. Sarah Thomas

*"What I'm learning from this is that it is possible to have it all.
You can have your cake and eat it too. But...
you can't have all the cake all the time."*

I remember sitting in AP Psych class during my junior year of high school, my mind wandering as usual. When I was younger, I would doodle to distract myself, but by that age, I mainly wrote. Short stories, poems, songs—you name it. On that particular day, I decided to compose a list, a note to my future self about what it's like to be a teenager, for when I eventually have kids of my own.

Fast forward several years, and I vaguely recalled that list, along with many other lists I'd written about my future life plans. I don't know what happened to those notes, carefully stowed away in my wallet, but it would be interesting to stumble upon them now. I'd guess that less than 10% of those plans have become reality, which, honestly, is probably for the best. However, one aspiration that has remained constant is my desire to become a mom and have a family.

In 2019, Erin Kiger asked me to contribute a chapter to her book, *Balancing the EDU* Life, where educators share their struggles and successes with work-life balance (I was also the book's publisher). I jumped at the chance, as Erin, like Barbara, is a great friend, and I am honored to be part of anything she is organizing.

While writing my chapter, my family life was taking shape in real-time. The chapter even featured a song lyric that became my mantra during that period: *"Instead of moving mountains, let the mountains move you"* (Skylar Grey). For years, I'd been "married" to my career, pursuing a doctoral degree and building my company, EduMatch®. When people inquired about my plans post-graduation, I'd respond, "Have a social life." And that's what exactly happened.

Long story short, I reconnected with an old colleague ("McDreamy," as he was known to my friends) at a workshop; we exchanged numbers, and the rest, as they say, is history. As I was working on the layout laying out Erin's book in 2021, she approved my update to the story:

As of December 2020, you can now officially call me
Mrs. McDreamy

Married Life

Married life has been incredible. My husband is an amazing human being. We have been through happy and sad times together, including our journey to grow our family. I'm a private person, so sharing this feels a bit awkward, but here's the link to my blog

I wrote about the highs and lows in 2022. Long story short, we started off our journey with heartbreak but ultimately were blessed with a beautiful, amazing little person. Despite the cliché, it was all worth it.

Now, a new level of juggling is in play: a toddler, a husband, a job, and running a company.

Recently, I've had to make some crucial, quick decisions and establish the following boundaries:
1. My family always comes first.
2. The future well-being of my family will always be a priority.
3. Self-care is essential for me to take care of my family.

Each of these could probably be a chapter, but in the interest of time, I'll just provide one example that encompasses all three.

The Why Behind the Shocking Hiatus

I refer to EduMatch as the "Magnetic Octopus," as it has so many different arms (social media, networking, podcasts, book publishing, non-profit, professional learning) that I hope will come together and support each other in time. They are starting to do so; for example, at the time of this writing, the 501(c)3 non-profit branch, EduMatch Foundation, Inc., is sponsoring an Artificial Intelligence (AI) summit hosted by the professional learning branch, EduMatch Professional Learning. I just came to the realization that EduMatch is actually *three companies* under one umbrella!

All that being said, different parts tend to be more active at different times. First, it was the social media branch, then the podcasts. When we started publishing books, this really took off! At the time of writing, we have released approximately 100 titles from educators and students. I am proud of this work and am so honored to collaborate with so many wonderful people who are willing to share their expertise and knowledge, including Barbara and some co-contributing authors. This has been an amazing ride, and we had lots of fun.

Last fall, I made a move that surprised many people. EduMatch Publishing was at its peak, an up-and-comer in the educational publishing space. We were starting to gain an international audience, and some of our titles were in high demand. So it shocked many people when, on 8th October 2022, I announced that no new titles would be accepted.

I explained my rationale in the email to the authors. One major reason is that our executive team had been talking for years about further establishing the professional learning branch and realized that we were unable to grow. Publishing is fun and rewarding, but it takes up a lot of bandwidth. It is a full-time job, and we were stuck, unable to move forward with our plans. One thing about EduMatch is that we pride ourselves on growing in line with the needs of our community. During the pandemic and remote learning, the education world shifted quite a bit in a very short time, which demonstrated a need for professional learning for many. We really wanted to help address those needs but had limited time and resources to do so.

Another reason aligns with the boundaries outlined above. I remember the day of the announcement, driving by a kiddie recreation center where I dreamed of putting my daughter into sports one day. What popped into my mind was, "But when will I have time to work on the books?" Red flag. We all have limited time on this Earth, and I want to spend mine building memories with my family. Working and making an impact is also very important to me, but again, we go back to the theme of balance. Author Brian Costello told me in an interview that life is never a true 50/50 ratio, and I agree. With, my family will always tip the scale.

Finally, mental well-being. This time taught me a lot about boundaries and learning how to say no. There were two periods when I found myself drowning; the first was after our pregnancy loss, and the second was during my complicated recovery after an unplanned Caesarean, being a brand-new mom. I remember that both times were very challenging but for different reasons. I needed to rest. I needed grace. I needed to give grace to myself.

I want to thank the EduMatch family members who gave me grace during this time. I know that waiting is not always easy. There were very few situations when I did feel pressured. Unfortunately, on these rare occasions, my mental well-being took a hit while it was already low from the healing process, whether physical, mental, or emotional. However, I am still grateful for these experiences because they taught me to establish boundaries and begin to let go of people pleasing (still working on that). I appreciate the low moments because they helped me to become a stronger person.

There's a lot more I can say about giving and receiving grace during the ups and downs, but I will leave that alone for now. The point is there were a multitude of reasons for taking a break.

Now that I've had some time away, I miss publishing. As I promised the authors, I have started creating resources that I shared with them on how to self-publish, and I am seeing the innovation and amazing work of so many wonderful educators. Kudos to Barbara and this project as an example!

I've heard plenty of people say, "If you love something, let it go, and if it returns to you, then it's yours," or something to that effect. Eventually, we will bring back the publishing, but with someone else at the helm. And I will continue to enjoy those swim lessons and music classes with my baby girl!

When It's All Said and Done

What I'm learning from this is that it *is* possible to have it all. You can have your cake and eat it too. But you can't have all the cake all the time. Motherhood, wifehood, educatorhood, and edupreneurhood (Hats off to Dr. Will!) are all different hats that I wear. Sometimes, they are stacked, but they are all part of my identity. Each has taken me out of my comfort zone in various ways and given me a new purpose. I'm growing in each domain and getting out of my comfort zone with new steps that I'm taking. Even as a company, we've taken a huge leap of faith with our pivot to pause publishing and focus on professional learning.

However, I'm reassured that it was 100% the right move, as I'm seeing our facilitators go out and make an impact. We are in the right place to help our colleagues navigate new topics, such as EdTech and generative AI so that they can help their students. Throughout this journey, there have been some growing pains, and I am almost positive that there will be more (hopefully not too many!). I am forever grateful to be able to learn and grow alongside amazing humans who inspire me to be better every day.

Thank you for reading my story! Here are some lessons that I've learned, which will hopefully resonate with you as well!

- Plan for the future but be open to pivoting! If you get a chance, reflect, and see what you can learn from the past.
- "Teamwork makes the dream work." EduMatch would be nothing without the community, and the leadership team works to bring their magic. Who is on your team? This can include family members and friends.
- Growth is great, but don't spread yourself too thin. Check to see what things you can streamline, automate, or pause to give you back some time in your life.
- Prioritize all dimensions of your health, including physical, emotional, mental, and anything else you deem important.
- Give yourself grace and expect grace from others in times of challenge. Consider this quote from Barbara, "We are human beings, not humans doing."

DR. SARAH THOMAS

Sarah-Jane Thomas, PhD is a Regional Technology Coordinator in a large district in Maryland. She is the founder of the EduMatch organization, which promotes connection and collaboration among educators around the world. Through EduMatch, Sarah has published several collaborative and individual books. EduMatch is also a recognized Google for Education professional development partner.

Sarah serves as President on the Board of Directors for EduMatch Foundation, Inc., a non-profit that supports the grassroots work of students and educators. In addition, she is a co-author of the ISTE publication series *Closing the Gap*, focusing on digital equity, as well as a Google Certified Innovator and trainer.

Sarah graduated from George Mason University with a doctoral degree in Education and a concentration in

International Education. She also holds a master's degree from Howard University in the field of Curriculum and Instruction.

Sarah was designated an ASCD Emerging Leader in 2016 and was recognized in EdTech Magazine's 30 K-12 IT Influencers Worth a Follow in 2020. In 2023, she was awarded Maryland Society for Educational Technology's *Outstanding Leader*.

Sarah was named by the National School Board Association as one of the "20 to Watch" in 2015. She was part of the Technical Working Group that refreshed the International Society for Technology in Education (ISTE) Standards for Educators in 2016-2017, and in 2017, she received the ISTE "Making IT Happen" Award.

Blog: https://sarahdateechur.medium.com/

Website: https://www.sarahjanethomas.com/

Twitter (X): @sarahdateechur

Podcast Episode #80:
Learning from Each Other to Inspire Others to Do the Same
https://bit.ly/episode80-thomas

17

3 Steps I Took to Go Out of My Comfort Zone to Create the Life I Always Wanted

EVO HANNAN

"Remember, your dream life exists, and if you can't sense it yet, you can usually find it somewhere outside of your comfort zone."

S tepping out of your comfort zone is a concept deeply rooted in personal growth and development. It can involve pushing boundaries, taking risks, and embracing uncertainty to achieve personal and professional growth. I think it's the uncertainty part that often puts people off from achieving their true potential. Being plagued by the 'What if it doesn't work?' and the 'What will people think of me?', and maybe the 'Is this really the right time to try this?' are ways our mind can play tricks on us to stay in our comfort zone and not reach for a new horizon.

I'll be honest: these were questions that used to be on my mind until I finally had a conversation with someone who was living the life I was dreaming of. This led to me taking steps (3 big steps) out of my comfort zone to create the dream life I have always wanted.

Inspiration, 2003

I have always been intrigued by the life of an entrepreneur. When I was traveling through an airport 20 years ago, I found myself sitting next to a guy with a business tag on his suitcase, working away on his laptop. I was intrigued by what he did for a living, so I sheepishly started a conversation with him. He told me he was an entrepreneur and was working on a project.

Back in 2003, it wasn't even commonplace to have a laptop, never mind a mobile. My understanding of an entrepreneur was limited to someone who creates a business from a passion, like one of my idols, Richard Branson. I was fascinated by it. You work on something you love with your own ideas, building a vision, traveling, and meeting people from around the world, and getting paid to do it. This was the dream. He told me about how he had transitioned from business to starting his own venture. He was traveling, making his hours, and choosing the projects he was working on. He told me with the right approach, niche, and ambition, I could do it too. I felt inspired, but it seemed so far away from the life of a teacher I had started just a year before. It was playing on my mind that I knew it was possible for me with the right approach.

Dubai, 2007

After graduating as a designer in 2001, I quickly took on the role to train as a teacher. This led to my first opportunity to teach Design and Technology at a local and very highly reputable school. It was both challenging and rewarding being the youngest member of staff on the team. Although I was one of the only members of staff from a minority population, I felt supported in my journey as a teacher and was given opportunities to express my creativity and share my passion for big thinking with the students I taught.

After teaching there for five years, it became clear that in order for me to progress into leadership, I would need to continue my career at another school. The school itself was such a reputable school that most stayed until they retired. With being one of the best schools in the area, I had two very simple choices: either move location to find another school that would continue to challenge me or move to another country. The latter seemed so much more exciting, so I read up about different places I could possibly teach in the world, reached out to some teaching agencies, and before long, I had an interview with a school in Dubai. This was a place that I had previously visited a few years back and was slowly becoming reputable as the Jewel In The Middle East. I was fascinated by its progressing growth, and after accepting the position, I moved to Dubai in August 2007 to continue my career as a teacher and start a new life as a big thinker. I distinctly remember people asking me where Dubai was and almost looking at me curiously as though I'd told them I was moving to Mars. Of course, then, it wasn't the tourist hub it is today.

Dubai is an extraordinary place. A different world. A Middle Eastern melting pot of all nationalities, visions, and religions, and somehow, it just works. Skyscrapers, ports, creeks, and authentic Arabian culture mixed in with beaches, shopping, and souqs, I knew almost immediately that I'd be surrounded by people who had bigger dreams, bold ideas, and sometimes objectives that seemed almost ridiculous to the average person. The act of moving your whole life to a city in the middle of a desert that was less than fifty years old was life-changing, if not a little crazy. My family certainly thought I was, but I always had their support. Especially my father, who had taken the bold step to leave his village in his late teens to relocate to the UK, a region of the world where he knew no one and knew none of its languages.

Dubai had started to become synonymous with bold and bright ideas. They completed the largest man-made island in the world in 2005, along with the largest man-made marina. When I arrived, they were in the middle of building the tallest building in the world, the Burj Khalifa, and had started work on the Dubai Metro, which would become the longest autonomous metro service in the world. By 2011 Dubai started to look towards its 50th anniversary and had started to create a mandate to become one of the most innovative cities in the world by 2021. This involved promoting innovation in all sectors, including education. This led to greater opportunities for me to push boundaries and promote big thinking in my classes.

Reborn, 2013

When my first child was born, everything changed. I saw the world from a different lens. Days seem to get brighter and full of opportunity. I was reminded of the conversation I'd had in 2003 and the dreams of being an entrepreneur. I felt a new drive, a new sense of purpose as I held my child and realised that everything I do will now directly affect his life. It was a feeling I wasn't going to ignore, and by his sixth month birthday, I started to think about new ideas that could help me grow both personally and professionally so I could become a better father for him. I started reading extracts from business books and understanding the importance of developing a professional network.

At the time, I only knew teachers at my own school and the neighbouring school. I knew I had to step out of my comfort zone and connect with more educators across the city. This led me to create my first brand, which would help educators in Dubai connect with one another at events across the city. I spent months perfecting the logo, brand, and its colours to ensure that it was being represented in the most professional and corporate manner. I took the time to connect with more people and partners to share this idea and to bring them on board. The first social event took place at the Dubai Marina Yacht Club in September 2014. We had over 70 educators turn up from over 15 schools across Dubai. The event was a great success and led to more events over the coming years, connecting more teachers across the UAE and, eventually, the Middle East.

This eventually led to a conversation about these events being highlighted in a Middle East Education magazine. It was like a dream come true and the first stage of feeling that my ideas were being validated by the wider world. I was not only learning and developing personally; I made some amazing friends along the way. This opened doors for more magazine articles and even led to a new career opportunity to lead innovation at a new school. As more doors opened, I found myself speaking at conferences about what I had created, which led to further engagements about my passion for developing networks and promoting innovation in the education space. I got invited to events, lunches and dinners; networking with more and more people, including some entrepreneurs who were a reminder of the dream I had of starting my own business one day. It was getting close; I had built up my confidence, grew my network and learned from my own venture I had launched in 2014. I found myself asking more questions and putting myself in front of more people to learn and grow.

Launch, 2021

2020 was a difficult year for all. The global pandemic left most of us wondering how and why we live our lives the way we do. Being in Dubai meant we couldn't visit our loved ones back home. It was also a time when I reflected on my own journey and where I wanted to be. I knew I had to start making moves toward ways I could start my own full-time business.

I started to create a business idea, develop a framework, and do some initial research, asking people in education about using my passion for teaching and innovation to drive change in the education space.

After making the decision to permanently return to the UK in the summer of 2021, I realised this could be a great opportunity to hang up my teaching jacket after 20 years and step out of the classroom to finally start my journey as a founder and entrepreneur. This was six months before the move, leaving me plenty of time to talk to friends and peers and prepare for what was ahead. I hadn't felt that level of certainty for a long time, it was a lot of change on many fronts in my life, but I was ready for it.

I registered the business 'Innovation X' and organised a soft launch event with a small group of friends at the Burj Khalifa. This was another way of me stepping out of my comfort zone and sharing with my inner circle my new journey, hopes and dreams. I felt inspired, loved, and supported, which motivated me to take things to a new level, and I started to connect, network, and strategise for the months to come.

I officially launched and started operating my company on 22nd August 2021 with no money, my eight-year-old laptop, and my network. Because of the conversations I had months leading up to the launch, it was the day I received my very first project, too, which was a great win for me, both personally and professionally.

This project led to more and more conversations, and before long, I was boarding the plane for my very first business trip to Edinburgh to support an online school with social media marketing and innovative projects through my first IX brand, Vertigo.

In the first year of operation, I got to travel back to Dubai, Edinburgh, London, and New Orleans. I also bought myself a new business phone and laptop. I was developing my own brands and projects and traveling the world. I was finally doing it, living this dream life that was inspired by a conversation with a stranger twenty years ago.

Live your dream, 2023!

Here I am. I've just finished my second year as an entrepreneur and celebrated the moment with all who have made a positive impact on my journey. One thing I have learned on this journey is the importance of surrounding yourself with people who believe in you. They will help keep you grounded whilst also inspiring you to think in new ways. They certainly have with me, and as I continue, I'll be celebrating both their wins as well as my own.

So, here's your opportunity to live your dream. Whatever your goals are, be patient, take the right approach, and make it happen. Remember, your dream life exists. If you can't sense it yet, you can usually find it somewhere outside of your comfort zone. So go find it, and good luck!

Evo Hannan

Evo Hannan is the founder of Innovation X, a big-thinking company that helps inspire a new way of thinking and reimagining education. Before devoting his work to Innovation X, Evo served as a Head of Innovation at several schools in Dubai and has taught Design for two decades.

Evo has been featured in several publications in the Middle East and UK and speaks about his passion for innovation and change in education across the world, as well as a two times TEDx speaker. He recently announced that Innovation X has worked in 3 continents, with 70 schools and over 25,000 students over the past 12 months. Evo is currently using his passion for education and innovation to drive change in schools through several projects, including Design4SDGs, Fusion, and Quest.

Website: https://evohannan.com/

Twitter (X): @EvoHannan

LinkedIn: https://www.linkedin.com/in/evohannan/

Rethinking Learning Podcast Episode #87:
Becoming an Agent of Student Agency
https://bit.ly/episode87-hannan

18

The Life-Changing Impact When Someone Believes in You

LIVIA CHAN

"Sometimes, it is easier to believe in ourselves when we know someone else believes in us first."
~ **George Couros**

First Surprise

A pril 2020 - Ding dong... knock, knock, knock. My ears perked up. I heard a thud that sounded like a large parcel dropped on the front steps and instantly wondered what it could be. As I opened the door, I saw an unexpected gift addressed to me by my feet. I looked at the unfamiliar name on the label, puzzled.

As I unboxed the package, my curiosity ran wild. Who was sending me a gift? I cautiously peered in to see what was inside.

Unexpected Gift

What was in the box? You wonder, too, don't you? It was something I never knew I wanted or needed until I embraced it for all it had to offer. It was not a tangible gift that arrived at my doorstep. Instead, it was a life-altering gift in the form

173

of an opportunity that led to one of the biggest changes in my personal and professional trajectory. It significantly improved my social connections, sparked a fire inside me to grow immensely, and inspired new passions in learning, writing, and speaking.

Since that fateful day, I physically felt a growing excitement in my body, mind, and soul that would develop into a deeper, joyful aliveness I had not experienced before. What is this brewing inspiration I could not ignore? It was an awakening of an evolving WHY that continues to grow today.

The Opportunity

This is the birth story of how stepping out of comfort zones led to deep connections, fulfilling empowerment, and the discovery and exponential growth of a NEW evolving why.

A stranger messaged (DMed) me on X out of the blue. I did not recall any interactions through tweets prior to this.

> Hey Livia, I hope you're well. I wanted to see if you'd be interested in joining us for an episode of our Teach Better Talk podcast. Any interest?

Apr 15, 2020, 7:12 AM

This was the first time I ever noticed his name. Now, his name is forever imprinted on my heart as an instigator of change, betterment, inspiration, and growth.

Jeff Gargas, the COO/Co-founder of the Teach Better Team, was the stranger. An invitation in the form of three sentences and a lot of courage was all it took to change my life's trajectory. If you notice the date, it was just shortly after the pandemic changed the world. I did not know then that my goals, dreams, and my world were going to expand exponentially.

At the time, I had not heard of the Teach Better Team. Distrustfully, I thought it was a hoax that Jeff reached out to ask ME to be a guest on their podcast! I was just learning to find my voice on Twitter months earlier, so why me?

The great thing about the internet is its digital footprint, so I quickly did some research. I checked out the website, reviewed previous podcast guests, and listened to a few episodes. It looked and sounded legitimate! I quite enjoyed listening to Jeff and his co-host on the podcast, Rae Hughart. Of all the 30,000+ people he followed and his followers, he chose me. "Seriously," I asked myself with even more disbelief, "Why me?" I am *just* a teacher from Canada.

After listening to Jeff speak on the podcast, he felt less like a stranger.

> Hi Jeff! I am so excited about this opportunity! Thank you so much for asking. I am looking forward to reviewing the GoogleDoc with the details. Enjoy your day!

Looks like a simple response, but this took a LOT of time for me to deliberate. "Should I? Shouldn't I?" Regardless, it piqued my interest, so I took the bait.

I am an introvert at heart. Even the thought of sharing my story in a small group, let alone the world, felt daunting back then. What would I have to say on a podcast that would be of value?

After learning more, I crafted my response. I must have read it at least 20 times. Each time, there was a steady increase in nervousness and excitement. Opportunities like this do not come along very often, so I knew my answer would be "yes". With my heart racing, I mustered enough courage to hit send.

> Hi Jeff, I am doing well. I hope you are too! Can you tell me more, please? I am interested. Thanks for reaching out.

Apr 16, 2020, 1:37 AM

By saying yes, something magical started to happen instantly. A joyful spark now lived inside, giving me an extra skip to my step and sunshine to my day. Jeff saw something in me. He believed in me. Every time I thought about this opportunity, I smiled because it warmed my heart. It felt like something amazing was brewing. I felt more alive with anticipation and excitement than a child in a candy store!

There is such energizing power when someone believes in you. I started to believe that I had a story to tell, or at least I better figure out what it was! Three months to podcast recording. I had time!

Follow My Heart

"Change is an opportunity to do something amazing."
~ **George Couros**

I've learned that I am someone who follows my heart. I trust it, especially when it is aligned with my thoughts. Sometimes, it leads me in directions I may not feel fully confident in yet, but I move forward knowing I can handle small steps.

Agreeing to be a guest on the podcast became an impetus for change. Truthfully, imposter syndrome knocked loudly at my door as I listened to more episodes and learned that many had more far-reaching credentials, breadth of experiences, or a web presence. Comparisonitis made me want to do more and BE more.

For years, I wanted to have my own domain name, but I never felt I had the time with my busy role on our Burnaby District's Staff Development team and my heavy involvement in ringette as a coach, player, and Executive on the board.

During George Couros's keynote at our local CUEBC conference in 2016, his call to action that resonated most was to reflect on our experiences through blogging. So, having my own website sat on my heart as a "one day when I have more time" bucket list item.

This was the perfect timing! The please stay-at-home pandemic with extra time to explore new passions led me to purchase the domain livchan.com. Excitedly, I set up my banner pages, and wrote my first post that night. It took me two days before I felt confident enough to hit publish! Not sure why it took that long because no one even knew I existed yet so no one would see it anyway.

Growing Confidence

Confidence begets confidence. The podcast invitation + pandemic shutdown + website development = awakening the small voice inside me to start sharing my story more often. I started participating in many Twitter chats throughout the week, which quickly grew my personal learning network. This allowed me to find my voice while sharing my story.

> *"All that we are is a story. From the moment we are born to the time we continue on our spirit journey; we are involved in the creation of the story of our time here. It is what we arrive with. It is all we leave behind."*
> **~ Richard Wagamese**

I felt so elated to know that the podcast episode dropped on 21st June 2022 that I wrote a linking blog post about my experience called "What Do You Do with an Opportunity?" Again, I felt that internal spark of joy and an excited aliveness.

Wow, my voice, and story are "out there" for anyone to listen! Is it possible that I could physically feel confidence grow in my heart and the burgeoning glimmer of a new WHY?

Soon after, I met more people from the Teach Better Team community and excitedly became an ambassador. I started writing more blog posts and was invited to be a guest on more and more podcasts. Each time, my confidence grew, and my belief in myself grew along with it.

Each invitation whispered, "I believe in you. You have a voice we want to amplify."

This was my journey to an evolving new purpose as an educational leader - one that would be farther reaching than in my own backyard. See how life can be transformed when someone believes in you!

Second Surprise and Unexpected Gift

Fast forward to February 2021—Ding dong, knock, knock, knock. My ears perked up. I heard a loud thud that sounded like a large parcel was delivered to my door. I wasn't expecting any orders. What could it be this time?

I brought the box inside. Deja Vu! Another gift? Looking at the label, this one stopped me mid-step. Gasp! My heart skipped a beat. My mind began to race. My brain could not believe what my eyes saw. This time, I recognized the name. I opened it with giddy excitement because it was from an Edu celebrity I admire and have been following for years!

It was George Couros, the same person who delivered the keynote I attended in 2016. He was one of the first people I followed on social media. As a role model, George consistently demonstrated authenticity and vulnerability. I continue to learn so much from how he openly and freely shares his views and experiences. Leading by example, George gave me a roadmap to follow - to authentically share what was on my heart and mind through blogging.

I received George's weekly newsletters in my inbox for years. One day, something in my heart tugged at me to say thank you for encouraging me to reflect through blogging. I was pleasantly surprised to receive a **response** that included a message about how he would follow my blog.

Shortly after and unexpectedly, George quoted a part of my blog post, "What Do You Do with an Opportunity?" in his weekly newsletter! George saw something in me. He believed in me. What an incredible gift!

> **"First step:** Open your eyes and your heart. Look around to see possibilities you can turn into opportunities. If you don't see one YET, you may need to take some initiative to find one or create one for yourself. Sometimes opportunities find you but you also can work towards placing yourself in situations where there will be more opportunities available.
>
> **Next step:** Assess whether these are opportunities you want to take. Can you grow from this? Does it help others in any way or make the world a better place? If so, then...
>
> **Final step:** Jump in or dive into the deep end! Take the opportunity! And if you are not quite ready, a toe-dip is still a motion forward."
>
> **Livia Chan**

If that isn't a statement that says, "I believe in you," I don't know what is!

Growing Opportunities

Opportunities beget opportunities. The more I shared, the more opportunities I had to express my thoughts, feelings, experiences, and stories.

A few months later, George called to ask me to be a guest on his podcast and to contribute a chapter to his book, "Because of a Teacher." Pinching myself, I had to make sure I was not in a dream! Since then, I have had other opportunities to share my story in other books as well.

Following that, George offered another gift that would grow in possibilities because of the belief he had in me. He reached out again to ask me to be a contributor to an online course on well-being. This would later ignite a passion and confidence to co-author a self-paced online course on Writing Strategies and author a course called Building Better Relationships on the Teach Better Academy.

All these opportunities eventually led me to the next realization that I love to inspire others in person and virtually through presentations as a speaker. My why continued to evolve because of the votes of confidence from others through many opportunities.

Three years ago, I would not have had the confidence to share my story, ideas, and writing in the way that I do now.

What's changed? It started with a bit of courage fueled by the belief that others had in me and, slowly, the belief I began to have in myself.

Over time, I began to understand that I am the teacher and the person I am today because I learned from others who freely shared their ideas. These thoughts and reflections inspired me to feel affirmed, to question, and to produce new ideas to share with others. I now have discovered I have a voice and one that is worth sharing.

*"When you hide your voice, you rob
the world of your creativity."*
~ Mrs. Smoot
(Dr. John Spencer's 8th grade teacher)

Growing Connections

Connections beget connections. I joined more Twitter chats, wrote more blog posts, and began attending the Administrator Mastermind group with the Teach Better Team. My PLN was growing, my voice was being valued, and my confidence grew*.

I believe in cultivating genuinely authentic connections. When I showed up as myself, invested in learning, and demonstrated care for others, this blessed me with deeper, meaningful relationships. The more people I met, the more I enjoyed meeting more people. There are passionate educators all over the world, and we found each other on social media and through the Teach Better Team.

How has this impacted my life? My two closest friends and many others live three time zones away! Friendships of the heart know no physical boundaries.

I thoroughly enjoy connecting, making new friends, and supporting educators from around the world. I never knew I needed a PLN family like this until I had one. I am better because of them. We are better together and stronger together. Maybe I am NOT *just* a teacher.

What I've Learned About Myself

My original life road map had me on a path to making an impact in the lives of children and families locally. Now that my eyes are opened, and my heart tugged towards more, I dream of making a greater impact in this world. With growing connections, increased confidence, and trajectory-changing opportunities, I feel joyfully alive every day.

Over the past three years since the pandemic, I discovered and learned that I have a voice. I have grown more courageous to use it and share it in all the circles I am in. I not only have a voice, I have a message. The more I share, the more I discover what my message is - honing it each time. I listen to what resonates in my heart to share.

I learned that I love people. The more people I meet, the more I love building relationships and deepening connections through my love and appreciation of them as gifts in my life. I love being inspired by people and their passions and the unique message they have for the world to learn. It brings me joy to pour into others and give my time and love. I'm learning more and more about myself each day as I am on a constant journey of evolving to be a better person through every atomic interaction. Each person adds to me - my heart, my brain, my soul.

Perspective is an interesting concept. When you learn or experience new things, the insight can be used to change your life's trajectory. If you invest in the opportunity, it grants you.

You are not *just* a teacher. You have a story and one that is worthy to be shared. Have the courage to step outside of your comfort zone and into your stretch zone. This is where you grow the most.

Here's How You Can Make an Impact

Believe in yourself.
See a possibility? Reach for it. See an opportunity? Take it! It means they believe in you. There is great influential power when someone believes in you first. If believing in yourself is a struggle, trust and listen closely to other's belief in you. Draw from and lean into it until you believe in yourself, too. That is enough to move forward.

Believe in others.
A few encouraging words and an opportunity can go a long way to change a life's trajectory. YOU may be the change agent in someone's life by saying, "I believe in you," or by providing them with that opportunity to shine.

Believe in students and all our children.
Offer that same gift to our students (and children at home) when we believe in them SO much that they eventually believe it, too. That gift can move mountains!

Whose life will you change today? Reach out and say,

"I believe in you!"

LIVIA CHAN

Livia Chan's true calling was to be a classroom teacher. Her journey led her to serve on the District Staff Development Team in Learning Technologies and is back in the classroom as the Head Teacher at Burnaby School District SD41 in British Columbia, Canada. There's so much more about Livia and the gifts she discovered.

Livia is a mother of two young adults and a ringette player and coach with multiple passions. Family and friends are at the top of her list, including people and relationships. Writing is one of them. Teaching, learning, and leading are as well, plus all things ringette!

"Working together to better ourselves, each other, and the world around us."

The quote above is Livia's tagline. It took her about three months to come up with something that reflected what she believed. We are not alone in this world. She believes she is who she is largely because of others around her who have loved her, guided her, supported her, and helped shape her being. Every interaction is an opportunity to make each other better.

Twitter (X): @LiviaChanL

LinkedIn: https://www.linkedin.com/in/liviachanl/

Blog: livchan.com/ **Class Blog** sd41blogs.ca/chanl/

Rethinking Learning Podcast Episode #120: Many Gifts to Discover
https://bit.ly/episode120-chan

19

Staying One Chapter Ahead

SHELDON L. EAKINS, PH.D.

If you can't fly, then run. If you can't run, then walk. If you can't walk, then crawl. But by all means, keep moving.
-Dr. Martin Luther King, Jr.

Introduction

This is my Grow story. After moving to rural Idaho, I was out of my comfort zone. Initially, this change of scenery and culture shock took me out of my comfort zone. However, I reflect back on the level of growth I have experienced. I'm grateful to live in this state, and I have learned a lot.

Five years ago, I attended a session, podcasting 101, and this was when I was trying to figure things out because I knew I wanted to create content. I wanted to learn how I can be better. The timing was perfect because as I was trying to figure out what was next for me, I stumbled upon this session, went into the session, and learned so much, and instantly, I was hooked. I was conversing with a principal the other day, and we talked about my experiences. I've done everything. I've taught elementary, middle, and high. I've been a school principal. I've been a director of special education. I've worked in higher education, and I've been in leadership roles. I've been a history teacher. That was my bread and butter.

I look through my professional career since I became an educator in 2008, and I've done everything. I've taught in urban, suburban, and private and been on charter school boards. I taught adjunct classes. This chapter will discuss what I've learned as a podcaster over the last five years. After all, as I said, I've done everything. However, I'm still on the journey and always trying to stay one chapter ahead.

Thankful for Idaho

I moved to Idaho seven years ago. I never thought I would. It was just not in my sights that I would become an Idahoan. It was funny because I just got my doctorate prior, and I was thinking, oh, you get your Ph.D., you're supposed to move into higher education. I need to be a professor, or maybe I need to move into the administration side. So, as a result, I started looking around for higher-ed positions. I remember my parents were living in Idaho, believe that or not, and I remember laughing at them like, yo, what are y'all doing? What are you thinking about moving to Idaho? But they seemed like they were enjoying it.

My dad really loved his job. He worked at the university and told me there was a TRIO job.

"It's right up your alley, Sheldon. You get to work with high school kids. You're used to working with students from limited income backgrounds. *They will be the first in their families to*

pursue a four-year degree. This is your stuff. You've done Upward Bound in the past. This is perfect for you." I remember responding, *"Yeah, but it's in Idaho though, like, there can't be no brothas out* there.*"* He said, *"just put it in. See what happens."*

Sure enough, I applied for a job at Idaho State University, TRIO, Educational Talent Search. Such a great program, but I messed around and got the job! The next thing I knew, I was moving my family to Idaho.

Moving to Idaho was More Than Just a Culture Shock

I grew up in Houston, Texas. So, the idea of moving to a very rural state, let alone a city, college town, small town, 40,000 people, we're talking. Honestly, I've gone back and forth with how I feel about this state. Now, I won't speak badly about the state of Idaho because I've learned a lot.

I remember plenty of times, especially when things were happening in the news, especially to my community, the Black community, police brutality, and other challenges. I was like, I don't have anybody to talk to. Finding a barbershop was tough. Finding the foods and restaurants, the type of things I was used to listening to radio stations, was challenging. I remember getting satellite radio for several years while living here because I couldn't find any music I wanted to listen to. The local radio stations weren't playing my jams.

Dealing with Challenges

One of the most powerful lessons that I've learned is that had I not moved to Idaho, the Leading Equity Center probably would never have started. I remember as an assistant director for TRIO Educational Talent Search; we had about seventeen different high schools that we served in our program across two grants. I remember visiting various high schools, working with the students, and listening to their shared challenges. Dr. Eakins, the teachers are telling us we can only speak English. The counselor said, speak English only Dr. Eakins, we got some of my classmates asking me, when am I going back to Mexico? Or Dr. Eakins, some of my classmates call me the N-word or other things happening.

That was on the student side. As a black man living in Idaho, I was dealing with my own challenges, microaggressions, implicit biases and discrimination, and flat-out overt racism. I didn't know what to do. I honestly didn't know what to do, and I said, you know what? I want to start creating content. I need to research. I was fresh off a dissertation, so I was still in research mode and needed to figure some things out.

In the beginning, a lot of the things I was dealing with, I didn't have a clue what it was. It just feels weird. It's a lot of subtle stuff. But I want to help myself. I want to help my students. Not only do I want to help my own two children, and I want to be able to share this with folks. So, initially I thought this place was not for me, but as I reflect over the last five years as a podcaster, my show would never have started.

The Leading Equity Center would never be around. I wouldn't have started online courses, a weekly newsletter called

The Weekend Voice Webinars, training, and a book Leading Equity: Becoming an Advocate for All Students. These things wouldn't have happened. So, I'm thankful for my time in Idaho.

I never would've been able to help so many people. I'm so fortunate and grateful for when I go on stage, go to a conference, or visit a school, and someone comes up to me and says, "Dr.

Eakins, "I listened to your show. Thank you. I listened to this episode, that episode, and I've listened to all your episodes. I feel like I know you, and I just want to thank you for the work that you are doing." These experiences would never have happened if I had not moved to Idaho.

I'm thankful for those opportunities. Over time, people started reaching out because I didn't think anybody was listening. I was checking my stats and saw my numbers were growing, but people started contacting me. "Can you do some training? We have teachers that need some support on culturally responsive teaching," or "we need some support of social-emotional learning," or "we need some instructional culture," or "we have a large population of indigenous kids. Our staff needs to figure out what to do. We don't know how to connect and relate, and we heard you work on a reservation. Can you support us?" The next thing I knew, I was starting a business. I initially ran away. It was Jonah. I ran away from the entrepreneur. I went into education because I grew up in a household where my father was an entrepreneur, and I said I didn't want to do that.

I want to know exactly where my checks were coming from. I wanted to know about health insurance, retirement, etc. I wanted that type of life growing up. So I went into teaching, but the next thing I knew, I got one foot in, one foot out. I'm still at the school working on a reservation. I'm doing the podcast as a side hustle if you will.

Life Happens, though. Right?

Now, if you've been through a divorce and you had children, you know, they're probably the ones that get impacted the most.

I went through a very tough divorce. I won't go into details, but it was a lot. And I got to a point where I needed to make a decision. I can either stay at the school I'm at and try to continue leading equity as a side hustle or not return to the school and pursue the Leading Equity Center full-time to be there for my kids.

My kids were young. It was tough, and I wanted to be there for them as a father. So I decided, you know what, for me to have the flexibility to be able to attend field trips, drop off kids, pick up my kids, be there for them through the summer, all these different things that I needed to do as a single dad, I decided to pursue Leading Equity full-time as I started doing training, you know, what was tough as a trainer, as a consultant doing workshops.

Impactful Lessons that I have Learned since Podcasting

The bottom line is you will never have everyone on board with any change initiatives. I've worked with organizational leaders, and they would tell me stuff like, we're ready for the training, but I just need a little more time because I want everybody to be on board. And I remember saying to folks, "Not everybody's going to be on board. Don't be 2, 3, 4 years from now talking about, oh, we're just not ready yet. Either you want to do this work, or you don't want to do this work, but don't lean on your staff and say, oh, the community's not ready, or my teachers still need to be prepared."

The next thing that I have learned is relationships with our students. The importance of relationships has become very cliche nowadays, but here's what I've learned about relationships and the power of relationships. They do not have to be cliché. I would never have survived as an educator if I hadn't put a focus on relationships.

Each student is different. Each student has their own needs. Each student relates to their own interests and topics, and if we don't take the time to create those relationships, to form those bonds, all we do is focus on the results with the mindset of "I need evidence that you have learned what I've taught you," and that's as far as we go and not consider the human side of our children. We're doing our kids a disservice, and I will put relationships over academics any day.

The next thing I've learned is how the media can sway folks' opinions and spark fear in us. As you're thinking about what's on the news today, there's so much fear nowadays about what I can teach, what books I can read, and what content I can bring into the classroom.

Teachers are afraid for their positions, jobs, and upward mobility—couple that with what happens outside of the classroom regarding social justice and other issues. Within the last three years, we saw women's rights, abortion laws, police brutality, and don't say gay laws. All these things are happening, and the influence, the power of influence of the media. A lot of conversations nowadays are surrounding gun laws and gun control. Like every other day, I'm hearing about another mass shooting. I always say this: when the cameras are off, does your mindset change?

Many folks will jump on board various social issues because they're being highlighted, but when the cameras go off, do we still care, or do we just move on or jump onto the next train? These things still happen. Police brutality still happens. Unarmed black folks are still getting killed. Our Asian communities are still being discriminated against. We still have kids down at the border. Our South American communities still face challenges. These things still happen, but if the media's not focusing on it, does that mean we must stop talking about it?

The next thing I've learned is that this work is still relevant and needed. I remember folks would say, you know, COVID brought on such and such. This work was needed before COVID. Here's the thing. The Industrial Revolution was from 1865 to 1900. During that time, education was managed from the top down, outcome-oriented, age-based classrooms, liberal arts curriculum, and a focus on producing results. Tell me, that's not what our schools look like today.

This work is still relevant. This work is still needed; if you aren't willing to do this work, who will?

Finally, the last thing I'm going to share as far as what I've learned over these last five years is that we need more voices that we aren't used to hearing. I remember five years ago, thinking to myself, "Man, I love listening to the podcast, but I'm not hearing voices of color. I'm not hearing from a lot of women. I'm not hearing a lot of representations from LGBTQ. I can sit here and complain, or I can try to do my part and provide a voice." I would come across many folks, especially many of them of color, who would start shows, but sometimes they would end up falling off. I wanted to be a consistent voice as much as possible.

So that's one thing that I've learned.

What's Next

I am still determining what's next for me. I don't know if I'll still be in Idaho five years from now. I'm planning to get a second book out. It's going to be about the sense of belonging. My goal is to continue to grow as an educator, as a keynote speaker, and as a facilitator.

We're all on a journey, and I love the quote from Dr. King and say it all the time. It's my favorite quote:

> *"If you can't fly, then run.*
> *If you can't run, then walk.*
> *If you can't walk, then crawl.*
> *But by all means, keep moving."*

We must keep moving.

Five years from now, this work will still be relevant.

SHELDON L. EAKINS, PH.D.

Sheldon L. Eakins, Ph.D., is the Founder of the Leading Equity Center. Dr. Eakins is also the host of The Art of Advocacy Livestream and the Leading Equity Podcast. Furthermore, Dr. Eakins is the author of Leading Equity: Becoming an Advocate for All Students.

With over 15 years in education, he has served as a teacher, school principal, adjunct professor, and Director of Special Education.

Sheldon Eakins is passionate about helping educators accomplish equitable practices in their schools. He has earned a BS degree in Social Science Education, an MS degree in Educational Leadership, and a Ph.D. in K-12 Education.

Email: sheldon@leadingequitycenter.com

Cell: 318-730-8204

IG: @sheldoneakins

Twitter (X): @sheldoneakins

Website: https://www.leadingequitycenter.com

Rethinking Learning Podcast: Episode #133: Discovering Your Journey to Advocacy
https://bit.ly/episode133-eakins

20. Taking a Year of Leaps that Led Me to Better Defining My Why and Path

STEPHANIE ROTHSTEIN 🌱

*"The most meaningful way to succeed
is to help others succeed."*
~ Adam Grant

W hen I was entering my seventeenth year of teaching, I had a conversation with my Associate Superintendent that shifted me.

"Have you ever considered getting your Admin Credential?"

"No," I balked. "That was never my plan. I love teaching."

"The best administrators love teaching."

I continued to tell myself I loved teaching for the next month, and while this was true, I also loved supporting teachers through coaching and chairing a Design Thinking Pathway. I found myself continuing to reflect upon that conversation. The scariest part of that reflection was that I really did feel solid in my plan of teaching until I retired. I realized that I gladly stepped into leadership roles placed in front of me. When a yearbook teacher retired during my second year of teaching, I took over; when asked to lead a new Design Thinking Pathway in my seventh year of teaching, I stepped up. While each of these paths taught me a great deal, I came to understand that these were choices needed but they were not fully my choices. The beauty of these steps in my journey is that they gave me the confidence to define my own why and path and eventually hear the advice of a trusted mentor.

The next month, I was invited by a parent of a former student to attend a Women's Leadership Luncheon, and one of the speakers was Diane Bryant, the former COO of Google Cloud. Diane spoke about how often she found women waiting to take leaps and pursue the next steps. I sat in that luncheon listening to Diane speak, and I felt I was put in that room so she could talk to me.

Enough signs had aligned, and I needed to listen. It was time for a change, and instead of waiting for things to come to me, I wanted to embark upon a year where I was the decision-maker in my own journey. This would be a year of my choosing, a year of growth, a year of leaps. I called this "A Year of Yes to Me," and this year changed me. As a proud Wife, Mother, and Educator, I do need to add one caveat to this story. Before I jumped, I checked in with my husband and my three children, who in 2019 were 9, 8, and 3, to get their thoughts on pursuing a path that may push me, make me uncomfortable and may honestly take me away from home more than we were used to. I knew that this meant that my husband, who already does a whole lot for our family, may need to do even more. We called this shifting from a 50/50 to a 70/30 balance for the year. Everyone gave me a resounding YES. So now, it was up to me. What had I stopped myself from doing or pursuing? What were leaps I told myself would be too big a strain? What did I want my next steps to be?

I began by applying to a summer cohort at Stanford School, and I got in! The focus of the cohort was to help you use Design Thinking in the classroom and to design your next steps. At the end of this training, I was asked one question, "What is your 'How Might We' statement?" A lightbulb went off in my head. The program had been wonderful, and I felt inspired to bring this work back to my school and my students. But this was not my lightbulb.

A few weeks prior to this cohort, I had read about another program called the Google for Education Innovator Program. At the time, the Innovator program had 3-4 academies per year in a variety of Google locations. They accepted 36 educators from all around the world. The big task of the application was to identify a problem in Education that you want to help solve and develop a 'How Might We' statement and a video explanation.

I immediately dismissed my chances of being accepted. Why would they pick me out of the millions of educators all around the world? Yet, the moment I was asked to develop my own 'How Might We' Statement, I knew that serendipitous moment was setting me up for my next step. While there were some steps to the application, and I felt intimidated by who else might be applying, I didn't let it stop me, and I applied to the upcoming Google for Education Innovator cohort in Singapore.

It was June 2019. I was with my children at our local Farmer's Market. My kids were messily eating and dripping snow cones on themselves, and it officially felt like summer. I feverishly checked my email for cohort notification. Nothing. A minute later, I checked again. Still, nothing. Then, at 3:55 pm, I got the notification.

Congratulations, Stephanie!

We are thrilled *to officially welcome you to the global community of Google for Education Certified Innovators. We loved reading and watching all of the passion, dedication, and ideas that were put into your application. It's clear that you are up to the challenge of working with your peers and with Google to drive school transformation in your community and around the world, and you have an important challenge to start with.*

You're Invited*: Google Certified Innovator Academy #SEA19*

I then called my husband. "You won't believe it. I got in!"

My kids had finished just enough of their snow cones to be able to chime in, "What did you get into, Mommy?"

"Mommy gets to go to Singapore!"

My kids immediately started telling everyone who was getting a snow cone, "My mommy is an Educator, and she gets to go to Google in Singapore!"

I stood there in the middle of the Farmer's Market and cried happy tears. I knew this was a leap that was going to change me.

A few months later, I was in Singapore, where I met 35 other educators from all over the world who wanted to impact education. The experience changed me. We went through Design Sprints, had coaches, and presented to people from Google who helped provide advice and insight about potential next steps. This experience helped me find my voice as an Educational Leader. It helped show me that educational challenges exist all over the world, and I was lucky enough to expand my network of those seeking to collaborate on solutions.

I returned from Singapore with fresh eyes, inspired to take on projects, make an impact, and seek out my next leaps. I was given the opportunity to partner with TED and participate in a course that supported Google for Education Innovators in learning how to give a TED talk. I decided this was an opportunity I wanted to say yes to. At the end of the class, I was chosen to give my talk in partnership between Google for Education and TED and was provided with feedback on ways to increase my impact.

Later that year, I gave my improved talk entitled "A Year of Yes to Me" at a local TEDx event. I am proud to say that it was accepted to go on the TED website. These moments, these leaps, and these decisions that were mine continued to propel me. Things were moving faster and faster; finding the path that was mine speeding things up.

After the TEDx talk, I began to share my writing and had a variety of articles and interviews published. I never thought about sharing ideas beyond my own school site, yet I came to realize how important it is to share my own voice. I partnered in projects with educators around the world and around the country and continued to share those experiences.

All of these helped me better understand my Why. I continued to come back to my How Might We statement, "How might we make education more collaborative and less competitive?"

My Why is my answer. I am here to collaboratively create impact. It is who I am in my family. It is who I am as an Educator. It is who I am as a leader.

I thought again about the question that my mentor asked me about earning my Admin Credential and decided that I wanted to do this my way. I did pursue my Administration Credential. In earning this credential, I decided that I wanted to seek out projects, opportunities, and next steps that would make an impact and bring me joy. I knew I wanted to approach my Educational Leadership work in partnership with others because I know that otherwise, we can never have sustainable change and make an impact.

I am now in my twenty-first year as an educator, and my current role is as an Education Innovation Leader in a K-12 District in Northern California. I support educators and students in deepening learning through innovative practices. I am one person, and there is no way that I will ever be able to create change at 30 school sites alone. I must collaborate and help to grow leadership, and this process should not be a competitive one. Helping educators and students grow benefits us all.

Questions for YOU

- Has anything stopped you from doing or pursuing something you've always wanted?

- Were there leaps that you told yourself would be too big a strain?

- What steps in your journey can give you the confidence to define your own why and path?

Instead of waiting for things to just happen, maybe it's time for a change. You can make that change happen.

This year could be your YEAR of LEAPS.

STEPHANIE ROTHSTEIN

As an Educational Leader, **Stephanie Rothstein** focused on making education more collaborative and less competitive. She is an advocate for modeling the risks we expect of our students and shared about this in her TEDx Talk "My Year of Yes to Me," published on Ted.com. In her 21 years in education, Stephanie has taught grades 9-12 English, Yearbook, AVID and chaired the LEAD Design Thinking Pathway at Los Gatos High School for 10 years. She is currently an Educational Innovation Leader for Santa Clara Unified School District, a K-12 District in Northern California serving 31 schools (K-12).

Stephanie's continuous love of learning led me to become a Google Innovator, Trainer, and Coach. She is a co-founder of

GlobalGEG, the creator of CanWeTalkEDU, and the author of numerous articles published on Edutopia and her blog. She speaks at educational conferences around the world and was named CUE's Teacher of the Year for 2021.

Stephanie is a proud contributor to "Because of a Teacher" by George Couros, published in 2021, and "Evolving with Gratitude" by Lainie Rowell, published in 2022.

You can connect with Stephanie on:

Twitter (X) and **Instagram** @StephRothEDU

Her website, https://www.StephRothEDU.com

Reflection #16:
Learning from Every Interaction and Opportunity
https://bit.ly/reflection16-rothstein

21

Leaning Into Our Growth

DR. RACHELLE DENÉ POTH

*"What students remember more than
the classroom is the community."*
~ Mayva Donnon

I have been in education for quite some time. I've now been able to look back over my career and reflect upon some specific times that have been impactful. While I enjoyed learning and sharing my knowledge with others, becoming an educator was not one of my career goals. After exploring options in college and because of a suggestion by my college counselor, I selected education as a major during my junior year at Penn State. I loved the student teaching experiences and opportunities to work with students, but I still didn't see it as a long-term career for myself. I thought that I would try it for about 10 years and then investigate other options using my French degree. However, once I had my own classroom, and I started to connect with students, it changed me completely. I was impacted by the connections made and the value in those relationships. That's when I knew I was here to stay.

I've always loved teaching, but I had different reasons for loving it. I enjoyed the opportunity to plan for the day, to share my knowledge with my students, to be able to interact with them each day, and have a chance to continue learning myself.

However, because of a specific group of students, I changed who I was as a teacher. I kept myself comfortable for a long time, using methods and tools that I was accustomed to and that had worked for me. I didn't think about changing things too much because it seemed that everything was working. The idea of trying something different was scary. I was afraid of failure and worried that if I did take some risks with new ideas or mix things up in my classroom, it would not go well, and that kept me from diving in. I stayed with the status quo because it kept me in my comfort zone.

But everything changed because of a group of students who got so excited about trying new digital tools in our classroom. They shared their excitement with me and with other teachers, which led me to apply to have them participate in a technology student showcase. When they found out that they were going to travel to the conference, they asked what session I was going to be presenting at the conference. And when I said that I wasn't, they challenged me. They asked me why I wasn't willing to take the same type of risk and put myself out there like I was having them do. I didn't have an answer. I never even thought about it. My goal was to have them be accepted to present and share their ideas and the impact with other students and educators.

So, we started with a state technology conference and that was in 2015. I remember that they had their student showcase first and that even though I had presented at a World Language Teachers' conference before, it was not anywhere near the size of this conference. When it came time for me to do my presentation, of course, my technology failed; the Wi-Fi didn't work, and the video would not play. I made some rookie mistakes and broke one rule that apparently everybody at a tech conference knows: Always download your presentation as PowerPoint slides or a PDF. My nerves had skyrocketed. I felt defeated, but I worked through it as best as I could, hoping that the hour would pass quickly and without any other problems. What got me through it was my students sitting in the back of the room, silently cheering me on, giving me the thumbs up, or making faces, that kept me going. More than anything, just knowing that they were there to support me made all the difference. That was a defining moment that then led to many changes and tremendous opportunities over the next five years for them and for me.

Diving in Together

It just took that first step to bring about so many great experiences and, more importantly, build the relationships between the students and our group. I had a group of students who would travel to some of the local and state conferences to present in the student showcase. Initially, they participated at this level, yet it didn't take long until I realized that they should also speak during my presentations. Having students step in to talk about a method or tool that we were using and giving their student voice to a room full of educators who needed to hear from them made a big difference. I needed to hear what they had to say. Student voice is powerful.

Each time we did this, my presenter role lessened because I wanted them to take the lead more. Through those first opportunities, friendships grew, learning happened, relationships became stronger, confidence was built, risks were taken, and above all, we embraced the power of learning, failing, and growing together.

That initial push led me to continue to seek opportunities to amplify their voice and the work that they were doing. Whether it was having them host a Twitter chat, contributing to a blog about a digital tool we were using, or even writing a chapter and some short stories in my books, everything that I did since that first conference experience required me to make a big shift. Sometimes, I am still not sure exactly how it happened, but I am glad that they pushed me to take a risk on my own. It shifted me from looking at what I needed to provide for my students and instead involved them more in saying what they needed.

I didn't go into my classroom thinking that it was *my* classroom. It was *our* classroom.

I didn't make all the decisions on my own. I had an idea for what I wanted to cover in class or for an activity. However, I wanted to know their input, and I wanted them to know that they were valued. The teacher I was before definitely valued building relationships with students, yet I did not see myself as a facilitator, a collaborator, or a co-learner. I saw myself as the one who had to make all the decisions and know all the answers. However, since that time, I have seen how much of a difference that risk-taking and looking for those opportunities made on me personally and professionally. Had it not been for that first conference and those students, I would have missed so many opportunities that have led to impactful changes in my classroom. There are many educators that I met during these conferences who have now become some of my best friends and motivators. Without them, some of the tremendous learning opportunities that I've been able to bring to my students would not have been possible. So, for me, what matters the most is finding ways to amplify others and also knowing that we need people to support us, too.

It never occurred to me why students were hesitant to speak up in front of their peers because, after all, they were their classmates. When I realized that I was asking them to do things that I wasn't comfortable with doing myself, that's when I knew that I had to change. I had to step out of what had been the status quo, keeping myself on the same routine and not trying anything different because I had not experienced anything different. Once I put them out there to embrace some risk-taking, they inspired me to put myself out there as well. When we connected through that first conference, nervousness, excitement, uncertainty, and pure awesomeness led to a truly supportive network and learning community.

A group of students who, in some cases, did not know one another and spanned different grade levels became supporters and encouragers of one another and of me. That learning network, that family we created traveling to conferences, sharing our knowledge and excitement for learning with others, made a difference in the teacher I was then and has continued to motivate me to keep improving and trying new things.

It's been years since that initial group graduated. Many have gone on to graduate college and finish advanced degrees; some are planning to get married and start families of their own. And for me, sharing those experiences with them, learning about one another, and forming our own learning and school family made a big difference in my life. I know that it did in theirs as well.

Wondering

Being seen, heard, and feeling valued is important for our students, and it's important for us as educators, too. Be willing to take risks and try new things even when we know we might set ourselves up for failure or lack the information and background that we need. When we surround ourselves with like-minded individuals or with people who are completely different, we will find a commonality between us, that is, in trying to improve ourselves and do better each day.

It takes that first step to break away from what you've always been doing. Take that step to venture into some new territory and extend your reach beyond maybe what you feel prepared to do. That's okay because that's the nature of learning and growing.

Remember that to do the best for our students and for us; we must surround ourselves with learning opportunities and supportive relationships. Creating a community in our classroom and connecting ourselves and communities outside of the classroom will bring about wonderful opportunities that impact not only us but our students and others.

DR. RACHELLE DENÉ POTH

Dr. Rachelle Dené Poth is an edtech consultant, presenter, attorney, author, and teacher. Rachelle teaches Spanish and STEAM: What's Next in Emerging Technology at Riverview Junior Senior High School in Oakmont, PA. Rachelle has a Juris Doctor degree from Duquesne University School of Law and a Master's in Instructional Technology. She has earned a second doctorate focused on Educational Technology.

Rachelle is an ISTE Certified Educator and a Microsoft Innovative Educator Expert. She is a past president of the ISTE Teacher Education Network and served on the Leadership team of the Mobile Learning Network for five years. She received the ISTE Making IT Happen Award in 2019 and has received several Presidential gold and silver awards for her volunteer service to education. She was named one of 30 K-12 IT Influencers for 2021. In 2017, Rachelle was selected as the 2017

Outstanding Teacher of the Year by PAECT (the Pennsylvania Association for Educational Communications in Technology, the PA affiliate of ISTE) and by the NSBA as one of the "20 to Watch" educators.

Since 2019, Rachelle has written seven books and contributed to many others. Her newest book, "Things I Wish […] Knew," includes the voices of 50 educators from around the world. She has also contributed to eight other books related to education.

Rachelle is a columnist for Getting Smart and a blogger for Defined Learning, Edutopia and NEO LMS. She has a podcast, ThriveinEDU, and hosts a PBL Podcast by Defined Learning on the BAM Radio Network. Rachelle is also a host of ThriveinEDU Leads a community of educators on Facebook. She presents regularly at state, national and international conferences and provides professional development and coaching for educators.

Website: https://sites.google.com/view/rachelledenepoth/
Blog: Learning as I Go: https://rdene915.com
Twitter (X): @Rdene915
Twitter (X) chat: #formativechat – Mon. evenings, 7:30 pm ET

Rethinking Learning Podcast Episode #70:
Taking Risks and Learning from Students Taking the Lead
https://bit.ly/episode70-poth

22

It Takes Two to Tango!
Tango Lessons and Life

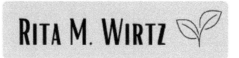

Those who can, teach. Those who can, dance.
To dance is to live. To live is to dance!

M y life journey has taken twists and turns. As the youngest of three, I was an overachiever growing up, expected to be excellent in everything, whether school, playing piano or dancing. I took ballet tap and attempted acrobatics, which was a no right away. I'm not sure why, but when rhythm was passed out, my dancing certainly lacked it. However, I excelled at the piano. My parents had the "idle hands theory"; we should always be learning or doing something useful. I had an older sister and brother as role models. Although my brother is gone now, I'm fortunate to still have my sister and a large extended family.

I always wanted to be a teacher. Going with my mother to teach adult non-readers was the beginning of a long career, including some years as a principal. I also had loving relationships with one life-altering exception.

Very few people knew I had two marriages. At nineteen, I married someone I thought would be my life partner. It was, in retrospect, a big mistake. Although, I stuck it out for two years.

We lived in Tempe, Arizona. I was finishing my degree at ASU (Arizona State University) in three years. In retrospect, I was always studying and that's likely how we stayed married. We barely saw each other. After graduation, we got jobs in a small town in Colorado on the border with New Mexico. I was teaching at the High School. He was a teacher at the Junior High.

My husband knew I was unhappy, yet he didn't want me to leave him. One day, after an argument, he tried to run over me, nearly hitting me with our Volkswagen bug car. I'm sharing this now because it was a huge part of my life journey. It took courage to tell my family that our marriage was a mistake. I finally left him. Actually, I escaped.

I finished up the school year and was having a great time teaching High School English, Speech, and Drama, sponsoring speech meets, debate, school newspaper and chaperoning for a church ski club. I was also taking classes starting my master's degree in Reading. As I think back to that time, as good as the good was, the bad part of my marriage remains a trigger. I don't recall ever mentioning to anyone what precipitated my running away from him and, at twenty-one, living on a farm with a wonderful family I had met. I am sharing that now because it may help someone else have the courage to leave a bad relationship or life situation.

Since we didn't have children, I gave him my wedding rings and all our money, and then I took off on a summer adventure

215

to recalibrate, including working as a hostess on a dude ranch. That summer, I didn't tell anyone where I was, including my parents. I was in full-tilt rebellion.

Then, I went home to Phoenix, found a teaching position, and began a totally different new life. I ventured into correctional education, working with teachers. This led me to a similar position in Sacramento, CA, where, a few years later, I met my husband, William. It was truly love at first sight, and in recollection, that formed the longest time in my life I recall being over the top happy.

I was twenty-seven when I married William, and, at twenty-nine, Rebecca was born. While my life purpose, my "Why" was always to teach, one position or another, my family was always a big part of my life. Family first.

I'm not happy that I had that first marriage, a major life goof. Fortunately, meeting William was the beginning of the best part of my life. We made our marriage work against several daunting odds. My husband was thirteen years older than me. We had other differences, religious and political. His mother really didn't like me at first. He already had three children, aged six, eight, and ten. I never had one worry we wouldn't make it work. Although I didn't think I could have kids, our daughter Rebecca was a surprise bonus.

Somehow, we figured out how to work as a team and discovered more commonalities than I ever imagined. To find a partner in life isn't always easy. To find someone I was going to be with for the rest of my life was remarkable. We were together for several years and then married for about thirty-six more. In that back-and-forth dance of life, we were inseparable. I was so blessed all those years.

We had a blissful, near-perfect marriage for many years until he passed away. During that time, I took care of him for six years. He's been my heavenly angel for over eleven years now. I've been starting over with places to live and with relationships for many years. It felt like my life was over. I kept thinking, how in the world could I survive without William?

My every breath revolved around him. When I look back at the family photos and trips I took with William, each one shows us clinging together, always touching, smiling, kissing, and loving each other. Even now, after being without my soulmate for so long, it feels just like yesterday. I vividly recreate scenes in my head of family dinners, outings, celebrations, and graduations. It took both of us to create a love-filled life.

We enjoyed music and dancing. We did fun dances like the Hustle Bump and enjoyed Reggae. William was a beautiful dancer, yet I had issues following him on the dance floor. I think I was so used to leading I forgot how to follow. I can't believe we never took dance lessons.

Whether on the dance floor or dance of life, it takes two to Tango, and a back and forth of sharing and caring makes a big difference. In fact, I've been taking Tango lessons for the past year, and I can assure you, it takes two to Tango. Yet William and I didn't Tango, and for that, I do have regrets.

Although we had fun fooling around on the dance floor, I would certainly do things differently now. I discovered I love to dance, and given the right music, opportunities, and partner, yes, I can dance. And sometimes, I danced well!

William and I created a destination resort or retreat for friends, family, and neighbors in the Tahoe area. When William died, I was left alone, hoping to start a wedding venue, but I couldn't get our 1856 house and property rezoned for a business venture. I finally decided I had no choice but to sell our house at any cost and leave. William had gone to U of O (University of Oregon) before law school, and our daughter Rebecca, my son-in-law TJ and granddaughter were in Eugene, Oregon. So many trips later, I moved to Eugene.

I discovered cool places in Eugene to hear blues and go dancing. I met a man, Hal, still a best friend, who showed me I do have rhythm and really can dance. There are many venues in Eugene to enjoy all kinds of music, but old-time blues really became my favorite. Dancing to blues music, with its special beat, was a revelation. Several times, my dance partner and I left the dance floor to applause. The first time, I didn't realize the applause was for us. Then it happened when we were dancing on a sidewalk, on grass, and a couple of times on gravel at an outdoor venue.

How in the world did I get involved with Tango at this later stage of my life? Again, my guy pal, Hal, who is a fabulous Tango dancer, encouraged me to go to dance lessons. Since Tango requires a close embrace, once the lockdown ended, Tango opened up, and I started to go to the Sunday afternoon dance lessons. My friend partnered up with me for several months, staying to practice after class. But Tango didn't come easily to me.

My buddy took me to have leather soles put on the bottom of my dance flats and gave me special powder so my feet could slide better on the dance floor. I have so many pretty pairs of dress heels, which would be ideal for Tango, but at this juncture, I wouldn't dare. I can't stand the chance of kicking someone or falling.

I took a few group classes and several private lessons at my teacher's home, and that helped. Then I caught Covid shortly after, so l lost momentum. For months, I was ill or recovering, so I didn't go to Tango class. When I finally went back, I was starting over pretty much every time. Adding to my dilemma, life kept intruding. Either I was ill, or my blood pressure shot up post-COVID. I keep injuring myself, tripping on things. It was too hot, too cold, pick a reason. The bottom line was in order to learn this glorious dance, I had to be at the classes. I was practicing at home. I really wanted to improve.

It seems obvious to me that although I have many gifts, Argentine Tango isn't one of them. I didn't give up, daring myself to be the best I could be, readily asking for help. As I watched the 'show' Tango, it looked so easy, yet I'm told by other students that it can take many years to learn.

In our journeys, there comes a time when we hit the wall, whether about a job, a move, a friend, a relationship, our health, finances, or whatever. It's at that very moment when we must decide whether to stop, back up, take a pause or move forward.

Last week, I hit that moment. I was back in class. Then I had missed several classes due to a family event and a Memorial weekend trip. So then, decision time. Here's what I wrote after making it to class. I'm planning to go tomorrow and hopefully every Sunday after that.

I'm just back from my Tango class. I was dressed right and had my dance flats and water bottle, but I was riddled with indecision. Have I failed? Me, the one who believes there's no failure, only feedback? In my head, I see myself gliding across the room. Our class is the real deal with our world-class instructor. I made my decision to go.

Earlier, Morgan, my twelve-year-old granddaughter, asked me if I enjoy Tango. I said, "Yes, mostly." She asked if I was the worst in the class. I said, "yes". I keep starting over because I've missed so much, and honestly, it doesn't come naturally. But I know this: today was my best day ever. I learned new steps and practiced where I was goofing up.

I know I am a better teacher than a learner. Tango helps my balance and calms me down. In tango class, I learn to give myself grace. Tango is just like life. Tango class students are kind to one another and me, as I am, indeed, the class project.

Tango urges me to pay attention to every detail. I must get out of my head and let it all go. I'll keep improving. Maybe soon, I'll put on my high heels, stay for the Milonga, dance, and spare toes of those kind enough to dance with me.

I encourage us all to take risks and learn new things, whether AI, maybe cooking a new dish, starting a relationship, or ending one. By not quitting Tango, I know that no matter what happens, I've given my all, not only by going but by trying to improve. Each bit of progress is a win for me.

Learning to follow as well as lead in my life has offered me perspective, humility, and the opportunity to discover an art form so pure and beautiful.

Near the beginning of the conflicts in Ukraine, amid shelling, couples were outside in the street dancing the Tango.

It's time to focus on this glorious dance of life, leading and following.

Let's all Tango!

RITA M. WIRTZ

Rita Wirtz served as Title I ESEA Program Evaluator in the California Penal System, Curriculum Coordinator for Sacramento County Office of Education, School Principal, Reading Instructor, K-Adult Teacher, and Special Needs educator. She shared her experiences as a Keynote Speaker and Seminar Leader traveling throughout the United States, inspiring other educators, and parents.

Rita holds a Bachelor of Arts in English and Speech, Reading Specialist, Masters in Reading, and Administrative Services Credential, pre-Adult. Because of her work with speed reading, she became a certified Hypnotherapist and NLP (Neurolinguistics) practitioner. Rita also studied "Brain Gym", a movement in learning.

Besides teaching, her greatest love is writing. "Writing is like breathing." She has written several books for parents and teachers, including "Reading Champs, Teaching Reading Made Easy (2014), and published her Memoir "Stories from a Teacher's Heart: Memories of Love, Life and Family" (2019). Rita's newest book is "Reading Champions! Second Edition, Teaching Reading Made Easy!" (2021).

As a featured blogger for Bam Radio Network's Ed Words, Rita brings fresh insights into the world of education and life. As of June 2023, there are 196 blogs to choose from and 12 mini-podcasts on tough topics affecting educators. Rita reflects on her accomplished career with humility and reflections on how all working toward common goals makes a difference.

Twitter (X): @RitaWirtz
FB: https://www.facebook.com/ReadingChamps/
Website: RitaWirtz.com
Instagram: @ritamwirtz
Podcast: "Let's Get Real" Bam Weekly Podcast
https://www.bamradionetwork.com/track/protecting-ourfreedom-to-teach-what-we-know-is-best-for-students/

Reflection #18: Why Teachers Are Leaving Now, Helping Them Stay https://bit.ly/reflection18-wirtz

23

Thank You Cards

FEDERICO JOSUÉ (JOSH) TOVAR

"You can't fake the funk with kids."
~ **Principal Kafele**

I alphabetized this month's thank you cards for our campus team members: Ms. Castillo, Mr. Chung, Mr. Ifurung, Dr. Luca, etc. The cards were from our Jaguars, which is what we call our students for the school mascot. I glanced at the students' comments and read the grateful words directed at their teachers.

Memorial Pathway Academy (MPA) established procedures to set up traditions that honor each other. At the end of each month, our Jaguars write thank you cards to their teachers. Our students recently arrived in the United States learning English as emergent bilingual students. Many of our Jaguars did not have a formal education in their native country so each classroom has different levels of academic understanding. Some of these thank you cards have misspelled "thanks" written in it. It's truly the thought that counts. The caring sentiment can be read as one person shows their appreciation toward another within that thank you card.

Creating an environment where writing these thank you cards is an established pattern of behavior that took time to develop. MPA's family makes the process easy for everyone.

Once our Jaguars write the cards during lunchtime, administration alphabetizes them and delivers them to their classrooms. As I organize these sets of cards, I smile and think of the struggles I faced when I walked in their shoes as a new immigrant to the United States in 1977.

I remember the traumatic experience of entering a new classroom in a foreign country with strangers speaking in a language that sounded familiar but not to where I could understand what was happening around me. My mom had forced my dad to immigrate and move our entire family and all our worldly possessions to El Paso, Texas.

Entering Ms. Cedillo's classroom, I was so out of place that I didn't even know how to write my name on my assignments. When I was a student in Ciudad Juarez, Mexico, I would use the nickname "Tito" on my papers. In second grade, my homeroom teacher said to me, "That's not your name; you are Federico Josué Tovar. Since most of your teachers don't know Spanish, we will call you Joshua (the English version of Josué). So, label your papers from now on, Josh Tovar."

I thought nothing of it because I needed to focus on basic vocabulary words since the Bonham Elementary administration had told my mom that I would be demoted from second grade to first or maybe kindergarten if I did not pass an oral vocabulary quiz by Ms. Cedillo. With the use of flashcards, I stayed in second grade.

As I continued to sort out the thank you cards, I found one card written to me by one of our Jaguars. The student wrote, "Le quiero dar las gracias por ser un ejemplo en la vida y por aveces contarnos de su vida y tambien le doy gracias por sus palabras que dice dia a dia y por sus consejos que aveces uno no quiere seguir, y por esos consejos son en seguir por que da una motivación a seguir. Muchas gracias por todo Mr. Tovar." Signed Y. Días.

In this thank you card, my Jaguar thanked me for being a role model in his life and thanked me for the advice I give daily during our morning announcements. He continued stating that many students do not follow my advice, but it's motivating and keeps him moving ahead.

As I reread this thank you card and thought about the words written to me, it confirmed all the notes I've received in the past with similar sentiments from previous students who I had a hand in supporting their learning process.

Memorial Pathway Academy is a special home located in Northern Dallas where all our Jaguars are At-Risk and require Tier III intervention. As a youth, I was that Jaguar and remembered the obstacles life placed in front of me as an immigrant to the United States. I needed to learn English using full immersion instruction, and being a child of divorce as a freshman in high school was abandoned by my parents at that point in my life. These events created a ripple effect over the years due to all my poor choices and the events surrounding my family that led to me not attending school and drinking a lot in the neighboring border town of Ciudad Juarez. That led to me graduating at the bottom of my class in 1988.

I have been in public education for three decades and have seen countless times how these kinds of obstacles destroyed many students or made them not aspire to many things in life. When I became an educator, based on my past experiences, I knew I needed to provide structure and care for my students, especially those who were walking in my shoes.

While attending high school, I had no connections with any teacher, no school pride and was drinking frequently. I was never an important cog in the high school system. I would hear about Student Council, UIL, Friday Football games, and SAT/ACT, but I was oblivious throughout my four years in high school to any of these opportunities that the "good" kids would take advantage of.

I met my counselor ONCE in four years.

One interaction went like this: I entered the office and sat outside in the waiting area. She came out, didn't ask me my name, but asked, *"What kind of diploma do you want to earn?"* I asked which was the easiest one. She heard that, said OKAY and sent me back to class. Many similar events are still taking place in today's high school factory system, where counselors have been turned into paper shufflers instead of focusing on the whole child.

One of my teachers in my junior year straight out told me that I would be a loser in life and would not accomplish anything. Crushing comments like that would destroy the morale of any student.

I was self-medicating and had no cares in the world as long as I had enough money to wash dishes at the Village Inn for my weekly alcohol binges. I knew I needed to pass my classes, so I would ask my teachers, "What do I need to do to pass this semester?" That semester rolled in with all the last-minute effort I put into different classes so I could meet the graduation requirements. As I had these small academic victories, I could not shake off what that teacher told me. I learned something about myself.

I learned I could use that toxic negativity not as a fire to destroy me mentally but as a fire that would push me to become a Phoenix and rise from the ashes of negativity. I learned that I had to stubbornly depend on myself since this loser had nobody rooting for him in life and at the schoolhouse.

Not understanding that the entrenched factory school system was not made to help students like me, a child of divorce who was an emergent bilingual who had more obstacles than supports. SEL (social-emotional learning), brain breaks, and cooperative teams were not the thing back then, yet teachers have always been the light of our society.

I felt as an educator, the system was failing too many students. Some educators who I studied under did not want to take responsibility for their actions of picking the winners and losers in their classroom, i.e. the class valedictorian or the rockers wearing a Mötlye Crüe cut-off jean jacket. These same adults didn't regret using toxic words like the ones said to me by my high school teacher.

> *"We might not like all our students, but the students should not know you don't like them."*
> **Rita Pearson stated in her TEDx talk**

Being called a loser, I knew where I stood with that teacher.

Creating a connection was something I had to learn over the years as an educator. It is a true statement that "hurt people, HURT people." I don't know if that teacher who called me a loser was going through hard times, but I do know that her comment directed at me was not how to connect with me or any student.

As educators, we are not in the science business, we are not in the math business, and we are not in the history business. We are in the people business. I learned one thing over three decades: kids don't care how much you know until they know how much you care.

Looking back on my high school experience, I feel that I would have gravitated to the high school experience if someone had connected with me. In Hispanic culture, adults use a term of endearment known as mijo/mija. I did more than the required seventy percent with those teachers who had the "mijo" vibe with me. I did attend their classes more because they were "cool" with me as a student. At the high school I attended, that was not the common practice from my experience.

The classroom teacher not only has to deal with the ABCs and 123s but with the emotional distress of the individual, like I did with my parents' divorce and abandonment. As a child of divorce, I can attest that it's a destructive event in the life of a student. This life event shatters most of my positive family memories. My beautiful memories of taking long family bus trips from Cd. Juarez to Mazatlán transformed into thoughts of why my mom would not fight for me and my brother during my parents' divorce.

When the process was final and my mom, Virginia, moved out all her items from the house, it was real. The non-stop waterfall of tears became customary as a freshman in high school. Contemplating this time in my life, I realized educators need to be able to look for the signs of deep pain. I also realized that the classroom I used or the campus I supported as an administrator needed to be welcoming for all students who face daily obstacles, such as emergent bilingual student(s), those children of divorce, those affected by drug use, or both. After

Virginia left, at night, I would be alone in my room, and I learned to tune out the thundering silence of an empty house by sleeping with the television on hearing the news. When I actually attended class, I didn't care about mitosis or meiosis. I was not looking to add or subtract integers and, for sure, I did not care about writing a paragraph. At the end of the day, I would return to an empty house and ramen noodles.

Universities spend a lot of time on Sergiovanni books, Lee Canter's assertive discipline program and lesson planning but never on how to deal with a child in emotional distress.

I began to understand how to nurture students by visiting my mom in her classroom as I began college. I loved her even though she did what she did to me. I knew she worked hard as a teacher with a caring way about her in her classrooms. My mom was also an immigrant to our beautiful country. She worked in a high school with many students who looked like us and brought the same struggles as emergent bilinguals. She was a teacher at Thomas Jefferson High School in El Paso, Texas, where she would educate many students who crossed the international bridge daily from Mexico to get educated in the United States.

The culture in my mom's classroom was unique. She would put up her students' work in her room. If she had student athletes, she would create a cut out of that student's sport and add their number and name on the cut out and place it in her room. These mijo (mija) actions created deep connections with her and her students. Now, don't get me wrong, Virginia, my mom, put up with no-nonsense and her students feared "the look."

You know… "the look."

She did not scream. She just would redirect behavior with her words and eyes. She once told me the moment a teacher argues with a student over an issue in front of other teenagers, that educator had just turned fourteen years old and losing credibility with the rest of her class. She said if other students would see you struggle and stop instruction, they would try a similar confrontation in the future to avoid doing work. She said from that moment on, you would be fighting over "power" in the classroom.

Virginia showed me a blueprint on how to connect with kids. As educators, we need to show them that we care, attend their activities when invited and do not argue with them over small things in front of their peers. The inspiring teacher or administrator will create a culture that students will love and appreciate. This will allow for connections to grow and have students willing to walk on fire for those educators who act on love and support. This kind of connection and school culture only develops academic success in a possible way. Any high functioning academic campus has a strong student-centered culture.

Entering the twilight of my career, I reflected on my past personal and professional experiences. I supported fourteen different organizations in three decades, from elementary to the university level. I supported organizations that were low performing all the way to the National Blue Ribbon. These experiences, along with the idea of building a positive culture, have solidified how I work with parents, students and team members. Regardless of zip code, financial status and other factors, educators who understand we are in the people business can create a safe place for our students.

"We need to connect with our students before they can connect with us. Once our students feel we have connected with them and they feel safe, there is no limit to what can happen and the glory everyone in that school can feel daily." Kevin Curtis stated in his podcast.

When I was honored to work at Socorro High School as principal, I knew that I was walking into the lowest-rated 6A high school in SISD with over 2,500 students. Socorro High School is in Socorro, Texas and is next to another international bridge with the city of Cd. Juarez. The campus had non-stop discipline issues, a rating of D- by the state of Texas, an eighty-three percent graduation rate, the climate survey was off the chart toxic, etc. I understood that we had to inject the campus with a steroid of positivity by making home visits, thank you cards, students of the week, sending students birthday cards, honoring A and AB students, honoring those "gut" students who increased from a 67 to 73, honoring our team members with breakfast, weekly meetings over donuts and the list goes on and on. All events were posted on social media so that parents and, most importantly, our customers and our students knew we were with them. We only wanted the good to be promoted along with their greatness.

Our Socorro team members and administration agreed that building a culture of positivity could and did make things better by acknowledging all our students who were academic giants or those who were like me, emergent bilinguals and/or going through emotional obstacles. At the end of my tenure as principal of Socorro, our family increased our rating from D- to B- in three years. The graduation rate increased from eighty-three percent to ninety-one percent.

These same practices have been brought to MPA. Our MPA team members are always looking to support our Jaguars with bell-to-bell instruction, a caring environment and a lot of the activities that took place at my previous campus. That thank you card my Jaguar wrote me and many others are in my binders of items given to me by my former students. At times, I look at their words, which truly make me know that our students are the inspiration. I will always remember sleeping in a dark room with the television on and thinking of the toxic words that spewed from that educator's mouth, and I will ensure that I do everything possible to have a safe environment for all. I will care for them as if they were my own.

I ask myself, as a dad, these questions:

Would I like to have me as a principal of my three sons?
Do the parents who drop off their children at MPA feel that I will care for them as my own?

"Is my school better because I lead it?"
~ **Principal Kafele**

The numbers and cards show that I am going in the right direction and always working to improve.

Educator, are you the champion that your students need? Are you the Linus blanket they need in a post-Covid era?

Tweet me at **@JTSpotlights** and let me know.

FEDERICO JOSUÉ (JOSH) TOVAR

Federico Josué (Josh) Tovar is a proud Team Member at Memorial Pathway Academy (MPA) in Garland Independent School District in Garland, Texas. He is an engaging, inspirational educator. Josh's focus is to create a culture full of love and joy for all students.

Federico Josué (Josh) Tovar believed that MPA needed to provide a safe environment and educate students, so they get to intermediate or advanced levels of English. He feels deeply that the school needs to make sure all students have a fighting chance when they go to regular middle or high school. Josh is also grateful that he works with educators who work miracles.

Twitter (X): @MPA_GOJAGUARS

Facebook: MPA Jaguars

LinkedIn: linkedin.com/in/josh-tovar-a7228623b

Instagram: @MPAJAGUARS

TikTok: mpajags

YouTube: JTSPOTLIGHTS

Podcast: @UnlockTheMiddle

Rethinking Learning Episode Podcast #142:
No More Orange Jumpsuits
https://bit.ly/episode142-tovar

Going Forward on Our Journey

BARBARA BRAY

*"Strength does not come from physical capacity.
It comes from an indomitable will."*
~Mahatma Gandhi

There was a reason that I used a heart-shaped tree for the cover. Every story really touched my heart. The contributing authors shared their journeys and stories that meant a lot to them about their reason for being here on Earth. There is a power in stories. The authors demonstrated that if we live on purpose, no matter where we are on our journey, no one can stop us.

When I started collecting the stories, I didn't realize I would be challenged with a life event: lung cancer. I knew I was having trouble breathing and had seen different doctors for almost four years. Each doctor's visit and with each test or scan, they said everything was fine. At least, we thought it was fine. Finally, I asked my doctor in April 2023 to humor me and do a CT scan. I then got that call: it was stage 2 lung cancer. What I learned is that you usually don't feel lung cancer until it's almost too late. I caught it early only because I had trouble breathing. In May 2023, they did a lobectomy (removed my lower right lobe). They got everything, and I healed fast. But...

I had to decide chemo or wait for 3 months for another scan. I have a great support team and wonderful family and friends who check often on me. Since I caught it early and there were no lymph nodes involved or other areas with cancer, I thought I could wait for three months. My oncologist mentioned a drug that would work. Yet, after doing genetic testing, I didn't qualify. I have atypical genes that are not covered for this drug by my insurance. Of course! I had to have atypical genes. Then, my sister, Sandy, found a clinical trial for this drug just for people with my atypical genes. Fortunately, this clinical trial was only a little over an hour from me. So that's what I'm doing.

I have to say I could be upset, worried, or angry, but I'm not. When I had the lobectomy, it fixed my breathing problem. That darn cancer must have been blocking my airway. There's nothing like being able to catch your breath.

I'm grateful that my sister found the study and that I qualified for it. I'm excited about each day now. When I had the surgery and needed to recuperate, I had to cancel events, conferences, and book signings for my book, Define Your Why. I also had to put off working on this book for a bit. It's amazing, though. I have energy now and decided it was time to clean my house and organize my life. I got together with good friends and decided to spend more time with my husband and family, especially my lovely grandchildren. I've decided to host my Zoom dance parties again.

Then, I received these inspiring stories from these amazing contributing authors. Each one touched my heart and empowered me to want to make this book happen. I also started getting invited to be on webinars and podcasts all about "Defining and Growing Your Why." Other groups wanted me to join their communities and do book studies. I do know that cancer sucks, but it's not going to keep me from being me. I have that "indomitable will" Gandhi quoted above. Yes, and dancing is part of my near future.

I had to be my own advocate to get what I needed for my health. All of us can be our own advocates for anything that may impact us. That's why I wanted to share these stories with you.

A few of the authors didn't feel confident that their story mattered. Many authors reached out to me that they had several stories and weren't sure which one to write. I really enjoyed meeting with the authors, listening to their stories and figuring out which one of their stories to write.

The stories they decided to write weave through multiple themes: learning from generations, understanding bias, creating systems of justice and equity, surviving through illness and tragedies, going through journeys to discover purpose, changing careers, being the best you can be, pushing oneself to try something new, and learning from all types of experiences.

Each story is unique and personal. I am excited that you got to this page which meant that you read the stories and learned about these amazing authors.

Everyone has a story. What about your story?

You probably have multiple stories and experiences that made a difference to you. Your stories do matter. Choose one of your stories and write it. Share it. Tell it.

"Find a subject you care about and which you in your heart feel others should care about. It is this genuine caring, not your games with language, which will be the most compelling and seductive element in your style."
~ Stephen King

Barbara Bray, an author, coach, speaker, story weaver, and difference-maker, has been on a mission for over 30 years to transform teaching so learning is authentic and meaningful. Barbara is co-author of *Make Learning Personal and How to Personalize Learning.*

As the host of the Rethinking Learning podcast and reflections, Barbara captures stories from inspirational innovators. These stories became the heart of her book, *Define Your Why: Own Your Story So You Live and Learn on Purpose* and now will be more stories as chapters in this book, *Grow Your Why...One Story at a Time.*

Barbara is invited to do presentations, keynotes, and workshops on growing your WHY through stories, rethinking personalized learning to empower learner agency, and disrupting the status quo. She is also co-host of the podcast "Real Talk with Barbara and Nicole" #RealTalkBN focusing on authenticity in a polarized society.

Barbara lives in Oakland, California with her husband, Tom. She has two children, Sara, and Andrew who both have one amazing, beautiful child each. Barbara loves being a grandma, spending time with family and friends, enjoying her garden, writing, listening to and sharing stories, playing games, and dancing.

Website: barbarabray.net

Why Press Publishing: whypresspublishing.net

Podcast: barbarabray.net/podcasts/

Twitter (X): @bbray27 #rethink_learning #DefineYourWhy #GrowYourWhy

Instagram and **Threads**: @bbray27

LinkedIn: www.linkedin.com/in/barbarabray/

Facebook: www.facebook.com/barbara.bray/

Real Talk Podcast: realtalkbn.buzzsprout.com

Other Books by Barbara Bray
https://barbarabray.net/books/

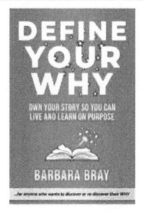

Printed in the USA
CPSIA information can be obtained
at www.ICGtesting.com
LVHW090348290624
784273LV00003B/355